DUI & YOU & ME

Save Lives

Mark William Lashley

ISBN: 1546508147
ISBN 13: 9781546508144

May 13, 2017

If you have ever driven after drinking alcohol or taking drugs of any kind, reading this book could save you thousands of dollars and save the lives of someone; maybe someone you know or love.

Maybe you are:

1. A Criminal and don't know it
2. A Danger to society
3. A potential murderer

If you, or anyone you know drives after drinking or using drugs, buying this book is **extremely important!** The cost to society is very high as a result of injuries and deaths resulting from people **Driving Under the Influence**.

This book is an educational, self-help, and inspirational story, all in one. It was written by Mark Lashley, who was a professional DUI counselor in the state of California, for more than ten years. He has taught thousands of DUI clients.

Mandated through the courts, they have paid thousands of dollars to attend these programs. Many of these people have said that if they would have known what they learned in these programs, they could have avoided getting a DUI.

Reading this book will teach you what is taught in most DUI programs, and hopefully you will never have to go to one. You can avoid being charged with:

1. Manslaughter or Murder II
2. Felony hit and run
3. Felony child endangerment

Included in this book is information to be able to assess whether you might be "at risk" for the negative consequences because of dangerous behaviors you're not aware of. Many people find out too late! You can prevent yourself and others from these problems. Reading this book can be a solution.

ACKNOWLEDGEMENTS

M any thanks to my special editors; Jackie, Donna May, Sue, Sandy, and my Mother. Also, to my brothers and sisters in the 12 step programs, where people help each other in the process of recovery... and the hope that is found there among the many broken hearted; working through a Higher Power to heal.

DEDICATION

To my beloved son David:
Whose life was ended in a fatal DUI accident.
Rest in Peace

CONTENTS

Acknowledgements   v

Chapter 1   DUI and You And Me: Resignation   1
Chapter 2   How to Avoid Another DUI   12
Chapter 3   Reducing Risk of Recidivism   27
Chapter 4   Why People Drink   36
Chapter 5   Progression of Use, Abuse, and Addiction   45
Chapter 6   What is Alcoholism and Addiction?   61
Chapter 7   Genetic and Environment Risk Factors   72
Chapter 8   Alcohol Effects on Body, Brain, and Behavior   76
Chapter 9   Changing Attitudes, Beliefs and Choices   82
Chapter 10   The Last Class: Madd Impact Panel   86
Chapter 11   Dark Night of the Soul   99
Chapter 12   Good News   120

About the Author   137

CHAPTER 1

DUI AND YOU AND ME: RESIGNATION

It was three o'clock on Friday when I decided to push the send button on the Email... giving my two-week notice of resignation as a Driving Under the Influence counselor. After teaching DUI School, for eight of my past 14 years as a counselor, I felt it was time to move on again. I needed a change.

Having been offered a job at an inpatient rehab, I had accepted the position. Back in 1999 I had worked at a rehab when I started counseling. It would not be easy. In fact, it would be quite a challenge. After months of considering this change, I pushed the send button on the office computer to notify management. I breathed a sigh of relief. This hard decision that would change the course of my life was made! The unknown was before me in this leap of faith!

Getting up from my desk, I slowly walked down the hall to enroll the new clients into the DUI program. This process is also a challenge. I get to be the welcoming committee, knowing that they are not exactly happy to be here.

Standing at the door to the education room where I knew they were waiting, I asked the front office DUI clerk, "How many new clients are here today?"

"There are nine. One cancelled and I re-scheduled them for next week." She paused and looked at me over her glasses and added, "Just to let you know, there is a person in there that is kind of upset."

"OK, thanks for letting me know." I took a deep breath and entered the room. Around the table sat 5 men and 4 women. Some were engaged in conversation while others sat quietly.

"Good afternoon and welcome to DUI School. My name is Mark. I will be assisting in enrolling you in the DUI program."

I picked up the stack of files to give them. I recognized a couple of them who had been here before. I called the names on the files and passed them out to each person. "Pleased to meet you," I said as I handed them their files.

One of the men told me that he wanted to talk to my boss. He was not happy about having to do the whole program again after almost finishing it the last time. Obviously very angry he stated, "It's all about the money anyway!"

I asked him, "Has it been longer than two years since you were here last?"

"I'm not sure. I finished all the groups and classes and thought I was done. Next thing I know, the cops arrest me for driving on a suspended license and they said I had a warrant out because you guys told the court I didn't finish. I lost my job because of this agency and now I have to pay for a new program and start the whole thing again?"

He was very upset and the new clients were waiting to see how I would handle this situation.

I took another deep breath, something I did often, and then replied:

"I will find your old file and take it to my supervisor on Monday. We can review what happened and we will figure out what options we may have. We can stop your intake for today until we consider it for you, or we can enroll you today and discuss this next week at your first individual session."

"Well, since I am here already, let's just do it."

I continued, "Let us open our files and start the process of enrollment. The first page is for personal information. Then we have a release of information for the Courts, DMV and probation department and anyone else you need to add. Next, we will fill out the payment contract and the client contract. We will then schedule your sessions. The whole process of enrollment will take a couple of hours or more. Any questions so far?"

They started filling out the forms. I took a sip of coffee and observed the new clients. You never know who will show up for a DUI Program. The whole spectrum of society is represented here. One thing is for certain: Most people are not too happy to be here.

I helped the clients fill out the information. One person asked me, "Where do I find the case number?"

"On your court referral, there is a case number, sometimes it is called a docket number. If you haven't gone to court yet, we can obtain that information later. We can enroll you with the citation or temporary permit given to you at the time of your arrest."

Another stated, "It asks for a license number and I don't have a license."

"You will eventually get an X number from the court that will be used with the DMV. We can also get that later."

I waited for them to finish the information form. "Now we will read through the contract together."

As we read through the contract, certain comments were made as we went over the sobriety section. "You mean we can't drink the whole time we are in this program?"

"No, you cannot be under the influence of alcohol or drugs while you are here on the premises. We have a zero-tolerance policy. If you are suspected of being under the influence, you will be required to be breathalyzed or give a urine sample."

One person asked, "You mean people actually come here after drinking?"

"Yes, that does happen. Also, if you drink the night before, you can test positive the next day when you come here. I have seen people get a DUI the next morning on their way to work. We will learn about the reasons for this in the education classes."

"What happens to a person if they test positive?"

"They will be discharged from the program and the court will be notified. Any time you are discharged, you need to get a re-referral from the court to re-enroll."

We continued through the contract. "If you are gone from the program for longer than two years, you must start the program over again. This is what may have happened to you." I looked at the client who was upset about this issue. "So, make sure if you are discharged, or leave the program for any reason, that you return before two years is up. Then you will get credit for the part of the program you completed."

We continued through the contract and the many reasons for discharge. When we got to the DMV form and the request for restricted license, many questions came up.

"When can I get my license back?"

I tell them to call the DMV to make sure what is going on. They need special insurance and must be enrolled in the DUI program. There are some things that the DMV requires for different people.

"Are any of you under 21?" Two people raised their hands. "You will not be eligible for a restricted license and will lose your license for one year."

One of the minors blurted out. "That is so unfair. I just got my license!"

"You will learn that driving is not a right but a privilege."

"What will a restricted license allow us to do?"

"A restricted license will allow you to drive to work, during the course of work, and to the DUI School."

I next inform them of certain new laws that they need to be aware of.

"You have a month hard suspension that starts one month after your DUI. If you had a valid license, you can generally drive for one month, unless you have a hearing with the DMV. Now there is a law that if you drive on a suspended license because of a DUI; you can be fined, have your car impounded and go to jail. When you get your license back, you will need to install a breathalyzer in your car. If you continue to drive while suspended, the fine and jail time increases each time, so it is not worth the risk. Arrange for transportation during the hard suspension period. You do not want to violate the Driving While Suspended law."

"If you are here for a DUI you received several years ago, the DMV may require that you complete the entire program before getting your license back. If you have any questions about your license, call the Mandatory Actions Unit of the DMV for information on your particular case."

Another person raised their hand. "How will the court know we are enrolled in the program?"

"We notify the court and the DMV that you are enrolled as of today. Remember to comply with all conditions of your probation. Check all those conditions on your court paper. You do not want to violate your probation. Most of you are on court probation and will probably never meet a probation officer unless you violate your conditions of probation. If you have community service to fulfill, or the DUI Impact Panel to attend, make sure you sign up for these requirements."

One of the clients asked, "I need to get an ignition interlock device installed in my car in order to drive again. What is that about?"

"In California, there are four counties that currently require an ignition interlock device (IID) for all first-time offenders. There are many states that require all first offenders to install this device. It was effective in New Mexico by reducing the recidivism rate for people getting another DUI, and has been initiated in California as a pilot program. This will become mandatory for the whole state beginning on January 1,2019. With this interlocking device, a person must breathe into the breathalyzer before they can start the car. It will measure any alcohol in your breath. It has proven to be a good deterrent for drinking and driving."

Another question from a client concerning this was asked. "I was not driving in any of those counties and I am required to install the interlocking device in my car. Why is that?"

"There is a new requirement for the Extreme DUI. If your BAC, which stands for blood alcohol content, or BAL, blood alcohol level is higher than .15, they have the authority to require a six or nine-month program and an ignition interlock device in your car. Extreme DUI were recently lowered from .20 to .15. What was your BAC?"

"I rolled my car and was taken to the hospital. They said I was .28."

"Yes, that is why. Were you injured?"

"I was in a coma and had head injuries. My truck was totaled! I don't remember much of that night."

"Well, I am glad you didn't die or have more serious injuries. Was anyone else injured?"

"Yes, my friend was thrown from the car and almost died."

The other clients had a shocked look on their faces.

"Were you charged with Felony DUI?"

"Yes, he answered sadly."

"We will now talk about DUI's that result in a felony. As in your case, bodily injury or substantial bodily harm to a person besides yourself is a felony DUI.

If there is a death resulting from DUI, the charge can be manslaughter or murder. The courts are now informing first offenders of the possibility of being charged with murder. One of the Multiple Offender's that we had in this program a couple of years ago, drove under the influence last year, killing a mother and her two children. He has been in jail for the past year charged with murder; because he had previous DUI's and had been informed of the new laws.

A fourth DUI within 10 years may be charged as a felony and a prison term may result.

Driving with a child 13 and under is a felony child endangerment charge. There are serious consequences in these cases. I have seen mothers who have picked their children up from school after drinking. Other mothers, smelling alcohol, suspected that these mothers were impaired, and reported it to the police. The impaired mothers were charged with DUI and felony endangerment of a child. These enhanced charges usually result in sentences of a considerable amount of time in county jail. I knew two women who spent almost a whole year incarcerated because of this behavior. Can you imagine the effects on the children seeing mommy arrested and being in jail for the holidays?

The state of New York has recently joined the majority of states by passing law concerning this behavior: Leandra's Law. A Father whose 11-year-old daughter was killed in a drunken driving accident pushed for legislation for toughening the law for driving with children in the car. His daughter died because of a mother taking his daughter and her friends to a slumber party. Seven other children were injured.

Leandra's Law changed the age of a child to fifteen and under. A person driving under the influence of alcohol or drugs with a child fifteen and under is charged with a class E felony, punishable by up to 4 years in prison, and a $1,000 to $5,000 fine. If a child is seriously injured, the charge is a class C felony, punishable by 15 years in prison. If a child dies, the charge is a class B felony, punishable by 25 years in prison.

The defendant must also register with the Statewide Central register of Child Abuse and Maltreatment of the state of New York. The Child Passenger Protection Act imposes tougher sanctions on individuals who place a child passenger at risk while driving under the influence of alcohol or drugs.

Automatic license suspension pending prosecution and the mandatory installation of an ignition interlock device for a period of 6 months are also required in New York.

California has a new pilot program requiring first-time offenders in four counties to install ignition interlock devices. If you get a DUI in Los Angeles, Alameda, Tulare or Sacramento counties, you are required to install the IID in your automobile or any car you drive or have access to.

Many states now require all first offenders to install IID's. New Mexico had one of the highest recidivism rates for people getting another DUI. As a result of requiring IID's for all DUI offenders, the recidivism rate decreased substantially. If this pilot program proves to be effective in reducing the recidivism rate for getting another DUI, California will join the other states in making it a requirement statewide."

One client raised his hand. "What is an ignition interlock device?"

"An ignition interlock device, or IID, requires the driver to breath into the mouth piece before turning the car on. If alcohol is detected, the car will not start and it will register the attempt in the system."

One of the young men in the group chuckled and remarked, "Well you can just have someone else blow into it for you."

I proceeded to tell them a story of what I witnessed when driving cab in San Francisco.

"I had finished dropping off a customer at the San Francisco Airport one afternoon. I stopped for coffee and sat in my cab in the parking lot. While I drank my coffee, a man parked next to me with two young children in his truck. He went into the supermarket leaving the children in the truck. While he was gone, a law enforcement officer parked on the other side of my cab and after getting coffee sat in his patrol car. Soon, the man exited the supermarket and under his arm he was carrying a twelve pack of beer. He put the beer in the back of the truck and opened the truck door. I was watching him give one of the children what appeared to be a tube from a bong pipe. The child put it in his mouth and I thought he was giving the child a hit of marijuana right there in the parking lot, with a cop watching too. The police officer ran around the front of my cab. He pulled the man from the truck, put him in handcuffs and then in the police car.

He called for backup and the man was taken away. Within fifteen minutes, a county van arrived and took the children with them.

I got called on another fare to the airport, thinking about what just happened. A week or so later, I was back at the same parking lot and saw the officer that arrested the man. I approached him and asked, "What was going on last week when you arrested that man in the truck with the children?"

"That guy had a breathalyzer in his truck because he had previous DUI's. He was having his 8-year-old son blow into the device because he had been drinking."

"Oh, my gosh! What happened to the children?"

"The children were taken by Children Protective Services. The man was charged with Child Endangerment and was sentenced to jail. He was also charged for his fourth DUI and will probably be in prison for some time." That was the first time I had heard of breathalyzers.

I continued telling the class about another call I would get as a cab driver. "Every Saturday morning, I would take a man to the liquor store to get his beer for the day. As I got to know him, he finally told me he had a car but could not drive it on Saturday mornings because he would test positive on the breathalyzer in his car. It was required because of his multiple DUI's. He said it was worth just paying me fifty dollars to take him to the store than risk violating his probation again and getting another DUI. He told me he got his last DUI on a Saturday morning after a Friday night of partying."

"When we do our class on blood alcohol levels, we will learn how the body metabolizes and eliminates alcohol and at what rate. That is something you all will need to know because if you are on probation for a DUI, you have Zero tolerance for alcohol. If you test positive for alcohol while driving, you are violating your terms of probation."

An elderly woman shuffled her paperwork and asked, "When can we start the program?"

"We are going to schedule you for classes starting next week. We need to get you into a class, group or individual session within twenty-one days."

Another person inquired, "Can we come every day to get it over with faster?"

"We cannot do that. The program must be the length mandated by the court or DMV. Are there any more questions? We can discuss any issues you may have when you attend your individual counseling session with a counselor."

Gathering the files from the clients I dismissed them. A few people approached me with questions and concerns. People are often confused in the beginning because of all the information presented. I answered their questions as I organized the files.

Another intake completed, I walked down the hall to my office.

CHAPTER 2
HOW TO AVOID ANOTHER DUI

Returning on Monday and sitting down at my desk, the countdown of only ten more days of DUI counseling became a reality. Finding the roster of the clients and proceeding down the hall to the classroom, I looked into the Multiple Offender group, recognizing past clients who returned with another DUI. I entered the classroom, passed out the roster and wrote on the board in big black letters:

Avoiding Another DUI

"In today's class, we will learn how to avoid getting another DUI. How many of you want to get another DUI?" Of course, most people don't raise their hands except the occasional jokers. Chuckle, chuckle.

"One of our goals through DUI education is to reduce the recidivism rate. Recidivism means getting arrested for another DUI. The recidivism rate is high for DUI: One out of three. According to these statistics, in this class of thirty, ten of you might be back for the multiple offender programs.

For many people, just being stopped by the police, handcuffed in public and placed in a police car is enough of a consequence to never drive under the influence again. The embarrassment and humiliation are enough of a deterrent. Some suffer shame, guilt and remorse that is unbearable. Do any of you feel that you are in that category?"

A few people raised their hands for this question. One woman explained. "I was arrested in my own neighborhood right in front of my house. The neighbors watched the whole thing. I have never felt so embarrassed in my whole life. The police put the handcuffs on me and placed me in the police car with my children also watching. I have never been in trouble. I have never even had a traffic violation. This is the worst thing that has ever happened to me."

I asked the class, "How many of you have never been arrested before this DUI?"

The majority of the class raised their hand.

"Maybe being arrested did not bother you that much for various reasons. Is that the case for anyone here?"

One young man raised his hand. "I don't remember being arrested. I was so drunk I woke up in the 'drunk tank' wondering what happened. I found out that I side swiped 3 cars and when the police arrived, I was passed out."

I asked him. "Were you or anyone else injured?"

"Fortunately, not!"

"How much did you have to drink that day?"

He shook his head and replied, "I don't remember. I was drinking all day at a barbecue and lost track. My BAC was 2.17, which is why I am in the 9-month program!"

"You are extremely lucky no one was injured or you would also be charged with a felony DUI. Did anyone cause serious injury to themselves or anyone else?"

Another young man raised his hand to speak. "I ran into a tree and my friend was seriously injured and is still in the hospital with a broken neck. I was also injured, but not as bad as my friend. I feel terrible that I caused this tragedy because of my drinking and driving."

I asked another question. "Did anyone experience a fatality in their DUI?"

No one raised their hand.

I continued. "So, all of you have avoided the extreme consequence of someone dying because of your DUI. The reality is that if we drive under the influence again and a fatality occurs as a result, we can be charged with murder and sentenced to prison. DUI judges are now informing First Offenders and having them sign an acknowledgement in court of the possibility of being charged with not only manslaughter but also murder. Injuring or killing someone is what I consider to be an unacceptable risk. Remember that Zero-risk of recidivism is our goal. We do not want repeat customers in this business."

Next, I write on the left side of the board:

How I Got My DUI

I ask newcomers how they got their DUI and write the responses on the board. I am always amazed at some of the answers I get from clients.

1. I was drunk!
2. I was in the wrong place at the wrong time.
3. I wasn't drunk; I only had a couple of drinks.
4. I was taking prescribed medications.
5. I ran off the road and crashed into a ditch.
6. I was not driving; I was sleeping in my car.
7. I got pulled over for speeding.
8. The cop said I ran the stop sign.
9. I ran into a parked car.

10. Someone called 911 and reported me.
11. I don't remember; I woke up in jail.
12. I don't remember; I woke up in the hospital.
13. I swerved to miss a cat and ran into a tree.
14. The cops pulled me over for no reason!
15. I was talking on my cell phone.
16. I didn't have my seat belt on.
17. My registration was expired.
18. I was driving with my lights off.
19. My tail light was out.
20. I was arguing with someone and the cops came.
21. I was escaping a dangerous situation and the police pulled me over.
22. Our driver was too drunk to drive, so I drove.
23. I got stuck in a DUI check point.
24. I was in an accident, but no one was seriously hurt.
25. I was in an accident with serious injuries.
26. I was in an accident and someone died!

People usually have some fun with some of the reasons, but with the last reasons given, seriousness covers the room. I pause in the silence and continue.

Next I write on the whiteboard the words:

Reasons people drove under the influence.

"Now I am going to ask you why you decided to drive under the influence the day you were arrested for your DUI. Do any of you care to share what you were thinking during this decision-making process?"

I wrote their answers on the board.

The first person said; "I didn't want to leave my car in that parking lot. What if something happens to my car? It might get stolen or broken into. My car is worth a lot of money!"

Someone else added, "How will I get to work in the morning if I leave my car."

Another said, "My friend offered to drive my car, but I didn't want anyone driving my car."

We discussed some of the reasons on the board. "OK, I didn't want to leave my car. So, what ended up happening to your car when you were arrested?"

"They towed my car to the tow lot and it cost me hundreds of dollars get it out!"

Another added, "I had to leave my car by the side of the road in a bad neighborhood and my hubcaps were stolen and my window broken!"

A young woman raised her hand. "I had to call my Father to help me get the car out of the tow lot because it was registered in his name. He was very upset with me. He said I should have learned from watching my brother go through this last year."

"Alright, what is another reason any of you used to decide to drive under the influence?"

I heard someone in the back of the class say, "I just wanted to go home and sleep in my own bed. My friends offered to let me sleep at their house, but I just wanted to sleep in my own bed. I needed to be home in the morning to get ready for work."

I asked, "So did you make it home and to work the next morning?"

"No. I had to sleep in jail and I got fired from my job because it was my third absence! Now I can't afford to pay for all of this. This has really caused me major problems."

A woman in front raised her hand and said, "I also lost my job because I have a commercial license that has been taken away for one year. I don't know what I'm going to do!"

I asked, "Did anyone else lose their job because of the DUI?"

An older gentleman said, "I lost my job as a delivery person because they can't insure me to drive the company truck. I had been with this company for twenty years!"

I added this reason on the list. 'I just wanted to go home.'

"OK, anymore?"

"I thought I was OK to drive. I didn't feel drunk."

"Yes, how many of you didn't feel drunk, and so didn't think you were drunk driving?"

Five or six people raised their hands on this question.

I added this reason to the list.

"Are there any other reasons people have to drive under the influence?"

"I didn't have too far to drive to where I was going, so I drove and… I almost made it there."

I wrote this reason onto the list and asked the class, "How many of you were just driving a short distance to go home?"

Many people raised their hands for this reason.

"OK, were on a roll, what other reasons?"

One elderly person told us, "I wasn't drinking. I was taking my prescribed medication and felt dizzy so I pulled over to the side of the road, and when an officer checked to see if I was OK, he called for an ambulance. They drew blood at the hospital and later charged me with DUI. I thought I was doing the right thing by pulling over. I am so upset over this whole thing. I have been driving for over forty years with no tickets, and now I have a DUI. I can't believe it."

I added to the list. 'I did not know I could get a DUI from taking my prescribed medications.'

"Thank you for sharing that with us. That is what they are calling: The New DUI. With the aging baby boomers taking many different medications, the awareness of being impaired while driving is something a lot of people don't consider. We are seeing more DUI's as a result of pain and sleep medications. Many other medications are resulting in impaired driving. It is very important to read the side effects of medications and be aware of how they may affect your ability to drive. We will learn more about this in one of our future classes. Does anyone have anything to add to the list?"

I looked at the list. "These are some of the most common reasons people give for driving under the influence. In order to avoid another DUI, it is important to understand the many reasons for driving under the influence. There are many other factors leading to our impaired driving. Alcohol and or drug abuse are common problems in the DUI population. Addiction also may be a cause for some. We will also learn about these problems next week."

I next wrote on the board:

PLANNING

I then asked the class, "How many of you are planning on never using alcohol or drugs again?"

Three or four people usually raise their hand. One woman stated, "I haven't drunk since my DUI. I'm too afraid to drink at all after all of this."

One thirty-something man told us, "My wife has been asking me to quit for a long time now. She said she would leave me if I didn't stop partying with my friends. I have been going to AA for a month now and stopped partying completely! I have two children now and I don't want to cause any more problems with my family. The party is over!"

I commented to his statement, "Yes, when the party is over and we get the tab, we can lose almost everything."

Continuing to the next part of the lesson, I asked the class, "How many of you are still going to use alcohol or drugs?"

The majority of the clients raised their hands to this question.

"So, for those of you who are still going to continue drinking and or using drugs, you need to have some plans for those occasions. What are some things you can do in the future to avoid getting another DUI?"

I started a list of their answers:

1. Have a designated driver.
2. Call a Cab.
3. Stay home.
4. Stay where you are when you party.
5. Just don't drive!
6. Call a friend to come get you.
7. Rent a limo with your friends.

"OK, these are some good alternatives to driving under the influence. Choosing a designated driver, as long as the designated driver doesn't drink, is a good plan. Sometimes the designated driver becomes the least intoxicated person, and can end up being the designated drunk driver. You need to choose someone before everyone starts drinking for this to be effective. Did anyone here get their DUI because of this failed plan?"

One young twenty-something man raised his hand. "A group of my friends went out drinking and we chose someone to be the designated driver. At the end of the night he was 'hammered!' We couldn't let him drive, so I drove. He was hangin' out the window when a cop saw us. I thought I was OK, but the breathalyzer reading was .09. I was arrested for DUI."

I asked him; "So looking back on the situation, what could you have done?"

"We could have called a cab."

"Good. That is next on our list. How much would it have cost to get a cab ride to where you were going, twenty, thirty, forty or more? How many cab rides could you take with the money it cost you for the DUI? You could have even taken a limousine and rode in style. It would be a good idea to have a cab company or two on your speed dial."

I glanced at the clock. I had time to tell the class one of my cab driver stories. "

I learned a lot about DUI when I was a cab driver in the Bay Area for 7 years. When I first started to drive for Yellow Cab, an older 'cabbie' took me under his wing after I got burned by a hooker for a fair in San Francisco. He was from New Jersey and had a heavy accent. When he said my name, there was no 'R' pronounced. It sounded like he was calling me 'Mock'. He came up to me in the cab lot early Monday morning after I was burned that weekend. He was always well dressed, well-groomed with nice Polo shirts and two toned shoes. His cab was always the cleanest, shiniest cab on the lot. His name was Spike. He put his hand on my shoulder and looked me in the eyes."

I began to tell the class about my conversations with Spike. "Hey Mock, I here ya' got burned last night. Look Mock, I feels sorry fer ya'. I been a cabbie for a long time. Do ya' wanna' learn how to make some dough in this business? I can help ya' out if ya' want. So, what do ya' think Mock, ya' wanna make some money?"

"Sure. What do I need to do?"

"Call me Spike," he said with a twinkle in his eye.

"OK Spike. What kinda' name is that?"

"Sicilian. My family's from Sicily and that's what they calls me. Any mo' stupid questions Mock?"

"No Spike, I appreciate ya' tryin' to help me."

With his hand on the back of my shoulder he kinda' guided me toward his cab.

"Now Mock, always keep the cab clean and polished. Ya' get better tips with a clean cab."

He cleaned a smudge off the window. Except for that small smudge, his cab was spotless.

"Now if ya' wanna' make money, ya' gotta get some peysonals."

"You mean personals?"

"Yeh Mock, peysonals. Them's is peoples that call ya' instead of dispatch to get rides."

"So where do I find these 'peysonals'?"

He laughed and jabbed me in the chest.

"Now ya's getting' it Mock. So ya woykin' next Satuday moynin?"

"Yeh Spike, I'm workin' everyday. I owe lotsa' money."

"Ok, good. So Satuday moynin' ya' go down to the county jail at seven. Ya' know that place?"

"Yeh Spike, I spent a few nights there over the years."

"It wasn't for a DWI was it Mock?"

"No, I never got a DUI. Why?"

"Cuz if ya' had a DWI, I couldn't let ya' drive my cab with my insurance. Ya' sure Mock?"

"I never have. I came close a few times, but I don't even drink at all anymore."

"OK Mock, So's ya' got busted a few times, no big deal, I was young dumb and stupid too ya' know. So be parked on the side street of the jail. At seven is when they release the peoples that got DWI's the night befo'. They will have a manila envelope when they walk out the door. Now they's gonna' need a cab ya' see cuz' they have to go to the police station and then to the tow lot and get their car, or somewhere else, so be parked on the side street of the jail. Ya' got some business cards Mock?"

"No Spike."

"Well, get ya'self some cards made, so's ya' can pass em' out, so's ya' can get them to call ya' when they need a ride when they lose they's licenses. Got it Mock?"

"OK Spike, I'll get some made."

"And Mock, let me give ya' another tip. When someone says to ya' they will be right back with the money, have them leave something in the cab so's they will come back and pay ya'!"

That week I got some cards printed. Mark's Mellow Yellow they said. I showed em' to Spike. He Looked at me with a grin and a chuckle and shook his head back and forth. 'OK, good enough, now start passin' these out so's ya' can get some peysonals'.

Saturday morning, I went and I parked next to the door where the prisoners were released. I thought about the times I walked down the stairs and down the hallway to those doors of freedom. From 'jailbird' to 'freebird'.

I asked the class, "How many of you have spent time in jail?"

Most of them raised their hand. Some had spent one night or two days. A few spent more.

At seven the door to the jail opened. A man holding a manila envelope walked over to the cab and got in. I could smell the booze on his breath. When you don't drink, you can really smell people that have been drinking. He got in the back seat of the cab and opened his envelope.

"Take me to the police station."

I drove to the police station in the next town over and parked. The meter read $12.00. He got out and asked me to wait for him. He came back 15 minutes later holding the release for his towed car. He looked at the meter.

"$18.00! When we got here it was 12 and we didn't even go anywhere. What's up with that?"

I explained to him that the meter keeps running even when the cab is parked. He was not a very happy guy. He probably had a hangover and a bad time in the jail that night.

"OK, take me to the county tow lot. I had to pay the damn police to get this release for my car!"

We arrived at the tow lot. The gates were locked and the sign said they were closed and to call a telephone number for information. He called the number and I heard him talking.

"What do you mean it will take you a half hour to get here! OK we'll wait, but hurry it up… I'm paying this cab driver with the meter running."

He hung up the phone and looked at the meter still running. It was now at $27.00.

"Can't you turn that thing off while we are waiting?"

"No, I have to keep it running for insurance reasons and if I turn it off the dispatch will send me on another fare. What I can do is give you my card and I will give you a discount. When you need rides in the future, you can call me personally."

He looked at the card. "Mark's Mellow Yellow. OK, thanks Mark. I'll probably need to call you if I lose my license, or if I get drunk at a bar again."

So that is how I got my first personal. I called Spike and told him I got a personal.

"Great Mock, now don't log off cuz' the peoples that left theyz cars are going to be calling for rides to go get theyz cars. Go get some coffee cuz yer' gonna be busy with these calls that will start when the drunks from the night before wake up and realize theyz left theyz car somewhere."

"OK Spike, thanks for the help."

After the coffee break I logged back on. My first call was to a suburb house. I parked in front of a house and a man came out on his front porch with his pajamas on and some coffee in his hand.

"I will be out in a few minutes. Go ahead and start the meter."

He obviously knew the deal of starting the meter while waiting. When he got in the cab with his coffee cup, he glanced at the meter and said nothing about it.

"I need to go get my car at the bar. I'm not sure which bar I left it at. I think it may have been at O'Leary's so let's start there. If it's not there we can go to the Red Fox. I think they threw me out of that bar so it might be there. I do remember that part of the night."

We drove around several bars looking up and down the neighborhood streets for his car. It was like doing a car search and the meter kept running, so I didn't care and he didn't seem to mind either. He told me it was a lot cheaper to pay a cab to go back and find his car than go through another DUI again. He said it cost him about $8,000 dollars for that DUI!

Being a cab driver I learned about what was going on when people got DUI's. There were people I picked up at the jails after getting a DUI and being arrested. There were people who had gotten DUI's and were not driving after drinking anymore, but calling cabs as an alternative. It was a real education for me, as I had never been arrested for a DUI.

I was starting to make good money driving cab with Spike teaching me. After about six months Spike told me he was moving to Las Vegas and he was going to give me some of his own 'peysonals'. He pulled out his black book and told me there was a rich guy in Hillsborough who goes to the city every Friday night, and it's a round trip fare. He gave me the address and told me; "don't be late".

I went to the address on Friday night 5 minutes early. I walked up to the door and rang the bell. A woman in a maid's outfit answered. I asked her if Mr. Rich lived here. She told me that he lived in the mansion behind the servants' quarters.

I walked around the back and saw the mansion with a gate and a phone. I called and he answered. He told me to wait in the cab and he would be out soon. I went back to the cab. This was definitely the clientele Spike had as personals.

Mr. Rich came out and got in the cab.

"Take me to North Beach in San Francisco and drop me off at Broadway and Columbus. Spike told you this is a round trip, right?

You will come back and pick me up around midnight, and don't be late."

In a half hour, we were in the city and took the Broadway exit. The meter was at about $50. I dropped him off in front of an Italian restaurant and decided to just hang out around North Beach till midnight.

As I waited, I remembered when in High School we came to North Beach for the first time. We were just 15 and 16 years old and one of our friends had the first car amongst our group. We were starting to drink on weekends and able to cruise around the city in his Volkswagen Bug. We would go down into the back alleys and peer in through the windows at the strip clubs. It was a huge thrill for us teenage boys.

That night my three friends, who already knew how to drink a lot, got totally drunk. When we were ready to leave North Beach none of my friends could drive and were barely able to stand up, especially the guy who owned the car. I was nominated to drive.

It was a rainy night and I was driving a car with a stick shift. I had only driven motorcycles, but never a car. As I managed to get us out of the city and past San Francisco State University. I was finally out of traffic and crossing Brotherhood Way. My friend who was passed out in the back seat sat up and saw me driving his car. He grabbed me from behind, told me he loved me and then hit me in the face and broke my nose. The other two friends were laughing as I tried to avoid crashing. We amazingly didn't crash and made it home. It was my first time driving under the influence and I was only 15 with no license yet. I was the designated 'drunk driver!'

Now at midnight, the personal client walked out of the restaurant. He was with a beautiful woman who looked like a showgirl. I opened the door of the cab and she got in first. I tried not to stare. Mr. Rich got in and I closed the door. I walked around the cab amidst the bright lights of Broadway.

As we drove down Broadway to the freeway entrance I heard her ask him why he wasn't driving his Porsche. He told her that the last time he drove home from the city he was arrested for a DUI. It was Halloween and he had to be in the 'drunk tank' with the weirdest people in the world. He told her he never ever wanted to go to jail again and would rather pay a personal cabbie $150 to take him back and forth rather than get another DUI. When I heard the money part, I realized that New Jersey Spike had a high paying clientele.

I learned about the DUI population by driving cab. Being a recovering 'drunk driver' who never got arrested for it, I never knew what was involved.

So here I was making money driving around 'drunk drivers.' Those who had been arrested and needed a ride from jail; those who needed to go on a 'car search' because they left their cars instead of driving drunk, and those who had DUI's and now arranged for transportation when drinking.

Which type of drinking person do you want to be? Calling a cab is much cheaper than risking being arrested for another DUI.

CHAPTER 3

REDUCING RISK OF RECIDIVISM

There are many reasons people end up in DUI School. Whatever the reason, they hopefully will learn from their mistake and not drive under the influence again. To prevent recidivism is the goal, in other words; not getting arrested for another DUI.

Unfortunately, people do get another DUI and the consequences can be devastating. Our DUI program has more Multiple Offenders than First Offenders.

We will examine some of the reasons for recidivism and the choices that people make to decide to risk driving under the influence again. The risks and consequences of another DUI vary in severity. The question is: are you willing to risk the possibilities of injuring or killing another human being, or yourself?

Hopefully, when people get a DUI, it will be a wake-up call. The problems vary in degrees of severity. Maybe they are just an occasional or social drinker. They might be an alcohol abuser, or even an "alcoholic." It could be the abuse or addiction to drugs; legal or illegal. We want to examine the root of the cause, whether it is bad decisions or habitual behavior.

DUI stands for driving under the influence of alcohol or drugs. DWI was the old way of saying driving while intoxicated. Some people still generalize by saying 'Drunk Driving.'

When we talk about drunk driving, I often ask people if they knew they were breaking the law when they drove and were arrested for the DUI. Some knew they were driving illegally as they were definitely drunk but drove anyway, thinking they could make it home OK. Others will say they did not think they were drunk and so felt OK to drive. Not knowing you have had too much to drive legally is common. It is important that people know what the law is concerning BAC levels and impairment.

The BAC, or blood alcohol content, is the measure of alcohol in your blood. When a police officer uses the breathalyzer when he pulls you over, it measures your BAC. A level of .08% is considered illegally intoxicated and illegal to drive in all states.

When I teach the BAC level and impairment education class, I would ask, "Who was .08 when they were arrested for DUI?"

In one such class a woman raised her hand.

"Did you know you were drunk driving at the time?"

She answered, "No, I didn't feel drunk at all. I only had two drinks!"

"Do you mind if I ask how much you weigh?"

"About 160 pounds."

I put a Blood Alcohol Content chart in front of the class.

"This is the copy of the chart the DMV sends you when they mail you your license. It is also in the DMV Driver Handbook. According to this chart, a female weighing 160 pounds could reach a BAC level of .08 after consuming 2 drinks. At a weight of 140 it could have been .09; at 120 it could have been .11 and at 100 pounds, .13. Now for a male of 160 pounds' weight it could have been .07; at 140, .09; 120, .10 and 100 pounds it could have been .12. Males and females differ biologically. Women have more adipose tissue, which are fat cells. Fat cells do not absorb alcohol, resulting in a higher BAC for females than for a male of same weight consuming the same amount of alcohol. Males have more muscle tissue which does absorb some of the alcohol."

One of the women said, "Well, that's not fair!"

"No, that's just physiology. There are other variables effecting blood alcohol content. As people get older the ability to metabolize alcohol by the liver is not as efficient. Having drugs in your system will also reduce the body's ability to metabolize alcohol. Medicines taken together with alcohol can enhance impairment and is very dangerous."

An older person in the class said, "I didn't even drink, I was on my prescribed pain medicine when I got my DUI."

I explained. "Driving impaired on drugs, whether they are prescribed or illegal is still against the law. Most medicines have warning labels about side effects. Some may cause drowsiness or dizziness. Always read the label and know how the medicine or drug affects you. The latest trend is people getting DUI's for impairment from prescription drugs. I have seen many for pain medications and quite a few from sleep medications. The latest studies have indicated that you might be impaired longer than the seven or eight hours of sleep time. Driving drowsy, either from lack of sleep and fatigue, or caused by medicines or drugs is very dangerous. Remember, you can get a DUI with a BAC below the legal limit if you are impaired, and without alcohol if you are impaired on drugs, legal or illegal."

One young man declared, "My BAC was .05, and I got a DUI!"

I asked, "Are you under 21?"

"Yes, I was twenty when I was pulled over. My drunken friend was barfing out the window right in front of a cop. It was his car and I wasn't about to let him drive!"

"So, what happened?"

"We both got arrested and our parents had to come pick us up. I got a DUI and my license was suspended for one year."

"Yes, the Zero Tolerance law for alcohol use is for all minors under the age of 21. It is illegal for minors if you measure a .01% BAC. You lose your license for one year, and if it is .05 or over it is a DUI. California also has a Zero tolerance law for anyone on DUI probation. How many of you are on probation?"

Less than half the class raised their hands.

I explained to the class the conditions of probation.

"Whether you know it or not, you are all probably on some form of probation. If you have been convicted in court, you definitely have probation of some kind. Most of you have court probation and will never see your probation officer, as long as you satisfy the requirements of your probation. If you do not comply with the terms of probation, you will hear from the probation department concerning your non-compliance.

Make sure you read the court mandates in your paperwork so you will know what is required. You can end up incarcerated and having your probation changed and lengthened."

I turned to the board again and underlined the words:

Reducing Recidivism

"So, now we will talk about how to reduce recidivism, or how to not get rearrested for another DUI. I have been a DUI counselor long enough to see First Offenders return as Multiple Offenders. Our goal is to reduce your risk of recidivism.

Let's look again at some of the ideas we came up with last week of how to not get another DUI?"

1. Have a designated driver.
2. Stay at home.
3. Stay where you are partying.
4. Call a cab.

5. Just don't drive.
6. Don't drink or take drugs.
7. Call a friend to come pick you up.
8. Rent a limo with your friends.

"OK. That is a good list. A designated driver is planning ahead, which is good to do. That plan works as long as that person doesn't drink and become the designated drinking driver. If possible, choose someone who doesn't drink at all.

The next one, drinking at home is a good idea. Make sure you have everything at home you need. After we have been drinking and our impaired thinking decides it's alright to go get some more supplies, we might think: 'The store is just down the street.'

"I knew a man in the Bay Area who drove two blocks to get a pack of cigarettes. He got a DUI on the way home; only two blocks. Every time he came to class he had those cigarettes and would hold them up and tell us how much those cigarettes had cost him so far.

In his first class, he declared: 'These cigarettes cost me hundreds of dollars so far because I had to pay the police to get a release to go and pay the tow truck company to get my car out of their lot. Then I had to hire a lawyer who wants hundreds of dollars to begin with! This is the most expensive pack of cigarettes I ever bought!'

After a month, he added the money it cost him to take a cab everywhere for the next month because he couldn't drive on a suspended license, after his lawyer finally lost at the Department of Motor Vehicles hearing.

The next month he added the court cost of $1600 after his lawyer lost at DUI Court, and his lawyer charged him more! And the community service he had to do was costing him to clean up the freeway with an orange jacket on. And to make things worse he was mandated to a nine month DUI program because his BAC was so high when he was arrested. By the time he graduated from the DUI program, he held up those cigarettes and claimed they had cost him thousands and thousands of dollars. He wished he would have just walked to the store that night."

Sometimes our plans just don't work out. There was another man who went through the First Offender program years ago. He graduated, and like all graduates, said he learned his lesson and would never come back as a Multiple Offender. I considered him to be at low risk of recidivism when he left.

A year later he was in the lobby when I returned from lunch to do my afternoon DUI group. I thought he was stopping by to say hello as some ex-clients do. I asked him how his wife and kids were doing and he said fine. Then he told me he had gotten another DUI! He said he knew we did not offer the Multiple Offender Program here, but he wanted to tell the First Offender group about how he got another DUI.

I went to ask the boss and she said it would be good for others to hear his story. We went to the group together. I introduced him to the group and he began his story.

"I went through Mark's First Offender Program about a year ago. I got my first DUI after a day of golfing and had several drinks throughout the day and one at the end of the game. I felt OK but when I was driving home I felt the effects and pulled over by the side of the road to rest for a while. I closed my eyes for a few minutes when there was a knock on my car window that startled me. I jolted and I didn't know my car was still in reverse, so when my foot came off the brake pedal, my car backed up into the police car behind me. The police officer smelled alcohol and arrested me. I don't consider myself to be an alcoholic and just figured I had made a series of bad decisions that day. I consider myself to be a social drinker and I drink a couple of drinks in the evening after dinner. I thought that if I just stayed home after drinking I would never get another DUI.

One Friday night I was safely home having a couple of drinks after dinner with my wife and one of my teenage daughter's left to go out with some of her high school friends. We were getting ready for bed when the phone rang. It was a call no parent ever wants to get; my daughter was on her way to the hospital in an ambulance after an automobile accident. I told my wife to stay home with our younger children and I would call her from the hospital.

My only thought as I started up my car was to get to the hospital as soon as possible. As I drove down the streets of San Francisco, I was finally in view of the hospital. It was then that I saw the blinking red lights in my rear-view mirror. The police officer stopped me and approached my car. He asked me if I knew why he pulled me over. I told him I was in a hurry to get to the hospital as my daughter was in and accident. He smelled alcohol and asked me if I had been drinking. I told him I had a couple of drinks during the evening. He told me to step out of the car and gave me the field sobriety test and asked me if I had ever been arrested for a DUI. I told him yes and he read me my rights as he put the handcuffs on for the trip downtown where I was breathalyzed and put in the drunk tank. I was allowed to call my poor wife. She called my lawyer and in several hours, I was released. It was the worst night of my life not knowing the condition of my daughter. She had a few broken bones and was going to be alright.

When I look back on that night, I could have called many friends or neighbors to take me to the hospital, but my only thought was to get there ASAP. Now I'm in a Multiple Offender group and just wanted to share my story and how we must plan for the unknown too. Have a plan set for emergencies just in case."

I tell this story to people in the DUI program because you never know what is going to happen. I received the same call about my son and one of my sober friends happened to be there to drive me or perhaps I may have also driven and been arrested for DUI too.

I once had a woman in DUI class who got arrested for DUI on a jet ski at the lake. The police took her to jail in her bikini. She didn't know it could be a DUI. They call it a BUI if you are driving a boat. We are seeing more and more BUI's these days from the waterways. The days of the party boats seem to be over as the waterways are heavily monitored.

There are some other ways to reduce recidivism that we have not listed. You can just leave your car at home so you won't be tempted to drive at all. You can also give your car keys to someone you can trust. Some people have actually bought breathalyzers that are now available at stores. As long as you realize your BAC could be going up after you test yourself.

Some people with an awareness of DUI have sleep-over parties and nobody leaves if they have been drinking. Guests can also surrender their keys when they arrive.

There was a public awareness program that used slogans to reduce DUI behavior. 'Friends don't let friends drive drunk.'

When I was still partying with friends at my house in San Francisco, we usually just stayed home and drunken friends would usually stay overnight. One night a friend, Big Mikey arrived late around midnight with a big bottle of vodka, and he was already drunk! About two o'clock he stood up very slowly and said he was leaving as he knocked over the chair and almost fell on the floor. My friends and I had never seen him this drunk and we knew we couldn't let him drive.

He stood in the middle of the room trying to get his balance. I asked him for his car keys and he told me 'no way.' I knew this was not going to be easy. I talked with my other friend and we decided that I would get on my knees behind him and my friend would push him backwards against the refrigerator. It worked and he landed; wedged between the wall and the refrigerator. He was like a big bear on tranquilizers trying to get up.

I tried to get the car keys out of his hand but he had a vice grip squeeze on them. With my friend holding him down I pried the keys out of his large hands and went to the next room to hide them in case he got up. He finally passed out till morning.

The next time he came over we told him we would get his keys at the door. We didn't want to go through that ordeal again. Big Mikey was the nicest guy in the world, but sometimes when he was drunk he could get belligerent.

Reducing recidivism can be a challenge for those who are heavy drinkers and tend to get out of control.

We will now talk about high risk thinking and situations that may lead to driving under the influence again.

You may decide down the road that you were just unlucky when you got your DUI. You were in the 'wrong place at the wrong time'. People sometimes don't consider the other part of that situation: 'With the wrong BAC or drug level'.

You may think that if you are more careful when you drink and drive you won't get caught again. You should have left earlier before the cops are out there and drive a different route home to avoid the cops.

When you start thinking this way you may end up putting yourself in high risk situations again. You might decide it's alright to go out drinking again if you just don't drink too much, and just wait till your alcohol level goes down before you drive. Once you start drinking you will be making impaired decisions and put yourself at risk for another DUI.

When you do manage to successfully drive under the influence again, you start to develop a pattern of behavior which leads to habitual driving under the influence again. You might convince yourself that it is OK; the first DUI was just bad luck!

Hopefully going through the First Offender Program will result in this being your last DUI.

Remember: Preventing recidivism is our goal.

CHAPTER 4

WHY PEOPLE DRINK

In the class topic for 'why people drink', we first discuss why people drink. I start by asking the class:

"Why do you drink?"

One young twenty-something man starts. "To get drunk"!

"I wrote this reason on the right side of the board in red. Are there any other reasons?"

A middle-aged woman adds, "To be social."

"Yes. This answer goes on the left side of the board in black. Oh yes, to be social. And at what type of social events do we sometimes drink?"

The same woman answers, "Luncheons. When I go out with my friends to lunch we all have a drink or two. I got my DUI leaving a luncheon in the middle of the afternoon. I usually have one drink, but that day I had two!"

"Do you remember when we learned about BAC levels and how two drinks can put an average woman weighing 160 pounds or less at .08 or more?"

"Yes, I should have stopped at one drink, but we stayed longer than usual, so I had one more."

"So, you learned that one more for the road was not a good idea?"

"Oh, definitely! Getting arrested in the middle of the day on a busy street was humiliating. I'm sure some people I know saw me being stopped and given the sobriety test. I can't believe this has happened to me!"

Next, I asked the class, "How many of you got your DUI with just two drinks?" Three women and an older man raised their hands.

I ask the older man what he drank.

"I had two drinks and I weigh one eighty-five. How can that be?"

"Well let me ask you, what kind of drinks did you have?"

"Long Island Ice Teas."

"Now those are not your regular standard drinks. Each one has more than one shot of different types of alcohol. Two of those drinks will definitely get most people inebriated. I used to drink those in my late twenties. One mixed drink like that could cause most people to get very impaired.

A standard drink is: A 1.5 oz. of 80 proof liquor; a 12 oz. of 5% beer, or a 5-oz. glass of 12% wine. Now if you are drinking liquor that is stronger than normal, you need to be careful because you may be drinking more than you know. Brands like 151 rums, Wild Turkey, and even stronger alcohol like Everclear can really impair you more than you expect."

One young middle twenties student adds, "Well if you are drinking to get drunk, those drinks work well. My friends and I usually drink to get drunk!"

I underlined this reason on the right side of the board in red. As I do this, another person says they drink to have fun. I wrote this reason on the left side in black.

"Yes, most of us want to have fun and be social. Let's talk more about the social reasons. At what other kinds of social events do people usually drink?"

I started listing their answers: Birthdays, weddings, barbecues, dates, parties, sporting events, get-togethers with friends, reunions, anniversaries, memorials, promotions and graduations.

"That is quite a list of social events. For people who just drink socially in moderation, these can be fun occasions. Now if you drink to get drunk, they can turn into embarrassing or even disastrous situations.

When I was younger my friends and I had a birthday tradition of drinking the same number of drinks as our age. This can be quite dangerous! There have been many deaths at college campuses where students would drink 18, 19, 20 or more shots and be pronounced dead on their birthday. Many college campuses have banned drinking because of these numerous deaths.

Weddings can be dangerous for some drinkers that normally don't drink. Low tolerance to alcohol can quickly affect people with small amounts of alcohol. We used to call such people, 'light weights'. And some people will arrive and start drinking champagne before eating and will be impaired before they even know it. You can usually spot these types of drinkers as they stumble around and even fall when trying to dance.

Weddings are also a good excuse to drink way more than normal for those celebrating this happy event. Social drinkers can get quite buzzed, and heavy drinkers feel right at home with plenty of booze available. When I was a professional musician in the Bay Area, we played many weddings where wedding cakes got knocked over before the cutting of the cake!

At one wedding limousines and cabs were hired to drive guests home to avoid DUI's or worse if they drove. I thought that was a great idea.

Occasionally, there is a wedding where there is no alcohol. It may be a religious reason, or maybe the people are in recovery or under age. When drinking is not acceptable, you may find a few guests partying in the parking lot or in separate rooms. When illegal drugs are used, they are usually done very secretly and discreetly.

Over the years, I have had clients who got DUI's celebrating or grieving over a divorce. I will write divorce in a middle column because it can cause people to react in different ways.

They may be drinking because of the depression they experience. I will put this reason on the right side in red. I have seen people that never drank until they went through a tough divorce. They might start drinking in excess and cause major problems, including a DUI, as they try to cope by drinking alcohol. Then on the other side in black, the person may be celebrating being free and able to go out and drink and party with their friends with no limits. I have seen people who were married young and never partied as they were raising families and busy with family life. After the divorce, they could change their lifestyle and do what they wanted.

You may have noticed the reasons on the left side of the board in black appear to be different than the right side in red. As we continue, the reasons people drink that I put in black, might be normal. The reasons in red could be very problematic for various reasons.

Now if someone is very shy and not very social, alcohol can be used to get rid of inhibitions. We used to call alcohol the 'social lubricant', or 'liquid courage'! Suddenly, you're able to talk to people easier and maybe even dance, or think you can dance. Alcohol may be your key to being more social. However, if you become too disinhibited, you may say and do things you may later regret, causing problems that were unintended in our right side of the board in red. Getting arrested and going to jail, doing community service and being in DUI class might be part of your new social life. Welcome to the world of problem drinking!

Sometimes, social drinkers can end up with problem drinker problems. I have also seen people who only drank and drove once and ended up in DUI class. There was a very small petite grandmother who came into my class and I assumed she was lost and looking for the doctor's office. She wore a breathing mask and had sanitary gloves on. I asked her if she was looking for the doctor's office and she told me no, she was looking for the DUI program. I told her this was the place and she put a chair in the corner away from everyone. When I asked the new people how they got their DUI, I called on her last. She took her mask off and shared her story with us.

She told us she was 85 years old and had never been in trouble in her life. She said her husband of 65 years had died last year. She had not driven at all in the last 50 years, as her husband always drove.

She took off her gloves and told us her friends in San Francisco invited her to their Widowers New Year's Eve Party. Living way out by the ocean, she did not know how to get there so she decided to drive her husband's Buick, which was in the garage. She made it to the party and had two drinks in the four hours she was there. When she left, it was very foggy as she drove out of the city along Golden Gate Park to the ocean side of town. It was very foggy and there were drops of fog water on her windshield. She was having a hard time seeing and did not know how to turn on the windshield wipers. A policeman pulled her over for driving without her wipers on and he said she ran a stop sign. He smelled alcohol and had her breathe into the breathalyzer. She was over the limit and was arrested for the first time in her life. She said she spent the night in the 'drunk tank' with dirty smelly people and thought they would all be here tonight, which is why she had the mask and gloves on. We laughed and welcomed her. She became the beloved grandmother of the DUI class. She was also an example of how someone who is not even a drinker can get a DUI their first time drinking and driving.

New Year's Eve is what we used to call 'amateur night'. It is the night that those who never drink and drive all year go out and try to drive.

Speaking of holidays; how many holidays do we celebrate that seem to require drinking?"

Someone says, "all of them."

"We have one coming up next week, Labor Day. This holiday we associate with the end of the summer time and the final vacations from school and work. It is in honor of all the working population and a time to have a three-day weekend of special events, and of course, drinking activities happen.

Then we have: Veterans Day and Memorial Day; Presidents Day and New Year's Day; Thanksgiving, Fourth of July and Super bowl Day. Also, there is Christmas, Hanukah, Easter and religious holidays of all kinds. We have a lot of Holidays that tend to be times to drink and party or celebrate.

Some of these holidays are known for high rates of Driving Under the Influence, and the resulting fatalities that result. The Law Enforcement Agencies are usually out in full force for these events. The Fourth of July is one of those holidays. People are out celebrating their independence and then they might end up being not free, but in jail!

We will talk more about Law Enforcement in another class.

Social drinking is a normal accepted activity. You may hear that drinking in moderation can be beneficial. Moderation is defined as 'two drinks per day' for men and 'one drink per day' for women. More than moderation negates any benefits, and, can possibly cause problems. Most of you may be here because of going past normal moderate use.

We listed many different reasons people drink. Another reason some people drink is because they are bored. Teenagers typically complain that they are bored and there is nothing to do, especially in the middle of the summer. When I was travelling as a musician, I would go into the club we were going to play in and after setting up the stage, I would go over to the bar and ask someone what there is to do in this town. Most people would say there is nothing to do except come here and drink!

Happy hour specials are daily events at bars for people who get off work and want to unwind and relax and be social too. Now if happy hour turns into happy 'hours' that may become problematic. You may end up drinking more than you intended. If you are drinking to escape problems, you might end up hearing the bartender yell out the two word sentences like; Last call, bottoms up, closing time, drink up, or just: 'get out!'

I'm going to put 'to escape' into the red category on the right side of our list, along with some things people are trying to escape. Someone said financial reasons. Most of us have financial problems. So, say you're drinking to forget your financial problems and as a result you get a DUI. What happens to your financial problem after a DUI? Not only do you owe a lot more, you now have legal problems added, and many more costly problems may occur.

Another reason listed is, "drinking to deal with stress.' The types of stress are many, including; work, money, school, relationships, family, loss of loved ones, loss of friends, and major changes in your life. You may have been promoted or demoted or fired or hired. Moving to a new location and starting in a new community can cause stress. We all must deal with some kind of stress in our lives. If you don't know how to deal with stress in a healthy manner, you may just try to drink away your problems, which is an unhealthy way of coping.

There are certain people that may be self-medicating depression or anxiety. Some depression may have a cause from something externally happening in your life, and some depression may be caused by a chemical imbalance in brain chemistry. People that are self-medicating are usually making the problem worse. Getting professional counseling or help from a doctor would be a better alternative. Depression and anxiety are often treatable with a combination of therapy and medications.

Pain is also a major reason people drink or use drugs. Alcohol is one of the oldest know pain relievers, along with morphine. I remember seeing those old movies where a wounded soldier was being examined. You would hear someone say that the leg has 'gangrene' and it must be amputated. Someone would go to the horse or jeep and get a bottle of whiskey. They would pour the alcohol onto the wound as an antiseptic, give the wounded a big drink, and then the man who was going to cut the leg off would take a big swig to steady his nerves. Alcohol was good for many uses. Morphine was also available as a pain killer in the mid-19th century. Because many wounded soldiers became addicted to morphine, it was nicknamed the 'Soldiers Disease'!

There are also other types of pain that people may be medicating. There is mental and emotional pain. PTSD, or 'posttraumatic stress disorder', may be caused by witnessing traumatic or terrifying events where physical harm or threats have occurred. Not only soldiers suffer symptoms such as intense fear, horror and helplessness, but victims of sexual or physical assault. Family PTSD can be present along with emergency workers and responders to accidents and disasters. There are many untreated PTSD soldiers, and others who are self-medicating ongoing symptoms.

People suffering mental disorders also may be self-medicating such as; Schizophrenia, bi-polar disorder, major depression, anxiety, panic disorder, and many other disorders that can 'co-occur' alongside substance abuse disorders. Some people may have multiple disorders occurring at the same time. Without professional help, these people may be at risk for many serious life-threatening behaviors and negative consequences.

There are also reasons many people choose not to drink. I have seen many clients who have stopped drinking after getting a DUI. Some are afraid to drink again, sort of 'scared straight', and some have high risk probation and are not allowed to drink at all. Others may stop to evaluate whether they do have a drinking problem. People with health problems may quit as suggested by medical professionals. Drug testing at places of employment with zero tolerance policies have motivated employees to not drink or use. When I worked for Yellow Cab, they had a zero tolerance for drugs and the .04 limit for commercial drivers caused many to stop drinking. Random drug testing in many companies require employees to immediately report to testing sites.

Many people have joined Alcoholics Anonymous after getting a DUI and are living a clean and sober lifestyle through 12 step programs. There are Judges who mandate 12 step programs as part of the conditions of probation. Certain religions forbid drinking and drug use at all. Other people just decide to quit because they have outgrown partying and it is no longer part of their lifestyle.

One of the goals of the DUI program is to educate people so they can evaluate their own drinking/using patterns. Then they can make the needed changes to improve their lives and achieve their goals, whether they are to avoid another DUI, or to stop drinking completely.

CHAPTER 5

PROGRESSION OF USE, ABUSE, AND ADDICTION

The next class in DUI is about the progression of use. I would draw a line across the whiteboard to represent the continuum of use from experimental to dependence. The starting point on the left would be no use, representing the time before we ever used alcohol or drugs. Next would be the experimental use. This is when we start experimenting with alcohol or drugs. I would usually start by asking the class: "At what age did some of you try your first drink or use a drug?"

One older gentleman responded, "I had my first drink when I was eight years old. My parents had a party and on Saturday morning I tried some alcohol that was left in one of the glasses. I think it was a rum and coke. It tasted weird, but I kinda' liked it. After that, I would always finish drinks that were left at my parents' parties."

"Thanks for sharing that. Did anyone start earlier than eight?"

A thirty-something lady raised her hand.

"Yes, what age were you?"

"I smoked pot with my older sister and her friends when I was seven. I drank when I started middle school, and continued to smoke pot after that."

Some of the clients rolled their eyes, maybe in disbelief or shock.

I then asked, "How many of you started experimenting in middle school." Several more clients raised their hands.

"How many of you started in high school?" More than half of the thirty people in the class raised their hands.

"And how many of you made it all the way through high school and started using in college?" Two or three raised their hands.

One client in his middle twenties told us, "I was into sports in high school and never used drugs or alcohol. When I went to college out of state, I started partying with some of the fraternity brothers. By the time I got out of college, I was drinking on all of the weekends after the games."

"OK, how many of you started much later in life?"

One middle aged lady raised her hand.

"Yes, how old were you?"

"Well, I didn't drink at all in my twenties and then I went through a divorce in my late thirties. I started going out with my single friends to nightclubs. We were leaving one of these clubs and my friends were too drunk to drive, so I drove. We got pulled over and here I am. I never even got as much as a speeding ticket my whole life, and now here I am in DUI School. I only had two drinks!"

"Yes, and we will learn how just two drinks can result in a DUI when we talk about BAC levels next week."

I went to the whiteboard and wrote the words:

Gateway Drugs

"Gateway Drugs are defined as the drugs of first use. They are alcohol, tobacco, marijuana, and inhalants. They are usually easy to get and therefore used in the experimental stage. Alcohol is a gateway drug, of which some of you already shared of your early use. Nicotine is another gateway drug. How many of you started out with cigarettes?"

One young woman raised her hand. "I smoked my first cigarette at eleven and have smoked ever since. I am now twenty-one and have tried to quit several times."

"Yes, nicotine is one of the most addictive and hardest drugs to quit. Some studies indicate that cigarettes are the main drug of first use. A study by the Substance Abuse and Mental Health Services Administration in the year 2000 indicated that young people who start smoking between 12-17 are 7 times more likely to use illegal drugs as non-smokers."

Another person shared, "I quit several years ago and it was very hard to do. First, I tried the patches, then the nicotine gum, then the lozenges. I tried the drug they advertise on TV and had some really bad side effects. I finally just quit cold turkey. I was very irritable for several days, and now I have been off nicotine in any form."

"Congratulations. Nicotine is reported to kill more people in the long run than any other drugs or alcohol combined. It is one of the most preventable causes of death. Now, how many of you started on marijuana?"

Four or five people raised their hands. An older gentleman said he was straight all through the sixties in high school and when he went to college, he smoked pot first, then drank and snorted cocaine while in his freshman year.

A younger man added, "I stole some of my Fathers weed when I was eight years old and shared it with my friends."

There was laughter amongst the younger clients.

I continued, "How many of you started with alcohol as your first drug of use?" The majority raise their hands.

I draw another long line and in the middle I will mark a point that indicates 'normal'. On the far right I will put another point representing 'Euphoria' and on the far left, 'Pain'.

Some people will laugh about the word 'normal'. They might jokingly say they don't know anyone who is 'normal'. I usually like to have a dictionary to refer to definitions. According to Webster's Dictionary, normal is:

1. Conforming to, adhering to, or constituting a typical or usual standard, pattern, level, or type.
2. Free from emotional or physical disorder.
3. The expected usual state, form, amount, or degree.

I relate to the class my first use of cigarettes and alcohol as an example. "My grandfather was a cigarette smoker. When I was a young boy, he would give me guitar lessons in his basement. It smelled like tobacco down there and he had several packs of non-filter cigarettes. Once when he was not home, I took a cigarette and went into the bathroom. The tobacco smelled good to me so I wanted to try and smoke one. I went into the bathroom and took a puff. I coughed so hard I thought my head would explode. It didn't taste like it smelled. It was a bad experience. I no longer wanted to smoke. So, what I learned from this experiment was that it was not pleasurable but actually was somewhat painful.

Now the next time I smoked a cigarette was in high school. I had a friend who smoked and he had some exotic cigarettes from Europe in a very fancy box and they were thinner and different colors. They looked good and I admired the way my friend blew smoke rings. It looked so cool I wanted to learn, so I smoked a cigarette and tried not to inhale. After a couple of puffs, I felt light headed and liked the feeling it created. I got a slight buzz. It was pleasurable this time so I kept smoking. I learned that it felt good and that I looked cool and felt older smoking with the smokers. We had to go to the special smoking pit over the hill from the school, as it was forbidden to smoke when you're under age. We were also breaking the law.

There were also some guys in the neighborhood who were sniffing glue in brown paper bags. We all went out to the cemetery. They put glue in the bags and covered their mouths while inhaling the fumes rapidly. They handed me the bag and I felt like I should do it since they all were doing it. I had sniffed gasoline with friends in grade school from lawn mowers. Inhaling the glue was a lot stronger and was kind of scary to me so I stopped doing it. I remember that one of the boys in the neighborhood did it every day and he started acting very strange. We think he suffered brain damage and his parents sent him away. It was just experimental for most of us, but it was addicting to our friend to the point of brain damage.

I remember the first party we had when we were in-between freshman and sophomores' years during the summer. We saved up our lunch money for a couple of weeks and one of the older brothers was going to buy beer for us. One of my friend's parents were going away for the weekend and so we planned the party. We had enough money to get the beer. It was a couple of six packs of Schlitz Malt Liquor.

Our friends garage had a camper parked in there which would be the perfect place for us to drink and not get caught. There were four of us and we drank three beers apiece. We had a radio blasting and went crazy and had great fun, until one of our friends got very sick and barfed up all the pizza we ate with the beer. It ruined the party and we had to clean up the mess before the parents came home. We were already planning the next party.

The next party of that summer, we saved more money and got a case of beer. If we had that much fun with two six packs, a case would be even more fun. Sure enough, we had the whole house when another friend's parents left for the weekend. We really got very drunk and had so much fun, except the same friend barfed again, but this time outside in the bushes. We just hosed him down and put him in the basement for the night. We really learned how to party that summer. When we started drinking hard alcohol we were experiencing bad hangovers, but it was worth the fun we had. We experimented with stronger alcohol like 100 proof whiskies and 151 rums and combined alcohols which really made us sick. We were experiencing negative effects, but not enough to make us quit. We were having way too much fun.

Our experimental use became social/recreational when we were sophomores. When there were football games and basketball games we would usually drink before or after, sometimes drinking beneath the bleachers or sneaking small bottles of liquor. Drinking at high school dances was risky and a few friends got caught and suspended. I liked drinking before the dances because it was easier to ask a girl to dance. 'Liquid courage' we called it. The benefits still outweighed the consequences. We were still having fun with alcohol.

I was also playing in a garage band in San Francisco when I started high school. A Grandmother of one of the musicians at the house where we were practicing told me something one day. 'The quality of your life will depend mainly on your attitude.' I wasn't quite sure why she imparted this wisdom on me, but I learned to listen to people that had been around long enough to have wisdom. Being a rebellious teenager at that time in the mid 1960's, may be why she told me this.

It is common knowledge that teenagers can develop an attitude towards their parents, teachers and authority figures. I am pretty sure I was one of those adolescents with an attitude. After all, it was the sixties in San Francisco. The culture of anti-establishment was a vital force driving the attitudes of the young generation at the time.

It was the second half of the sixties. The counter/culture was definitely influencing the young students in the high school where I attended. And of course, alcohol was an accepted part of the American cultural experience. In high school, it was illegal for minors to drink, but it did happen. We could always score alcohol somehow. There were siblings and older students who matured and appeared much older than they were. The liquor stores that would readily sell to minors with fake ID's were known. Certain students would just steal the booze from the store or their parents. Where there was a will, there was a way; as the saying goes.

Our attitude back then was; Alcohol is fun and it is cool and grown-up to drink. Hangovers happen, but it is worth it.

Our beliefs were also being formed from our experiences. One definition of beliefs in the dictionary is: A state or habit of mind in which trust, confidence or reliance is placed in some person or thing.

Peer pressure definitely fed into our belief systems. When older or more experienced students told us it was OK to do something, we tended to trust their confidence that it was alright. After all, they had tried it and guaranteed it was good. And after we tried it and nothing really bad happened, it must be true, right?

In the mid 60's we were turning 16 and anxious to get a driver's license. We were soon at the age of being eligible for getting a driver's license, and automobiles would be part of our lives. One requirement was to take Drivers Ed Class.

I remember our teacher. He told us the first day of class, 'There are thirty of you students in this class. Before you graduate from high school, one or two of you will most likely in probability die before then due to drinking and driving. Some of you might get seriously injured. Driving is dangerous anyway, and we need to learn to drive safely and never drive under the influence. You are all in the High-Risk population of society for fatalities due to automobile accidents, and driving while intoxicated raises that risk.'

One of the boys laughed. The teacher sternly gave him the most serious look imaginable.

'With an attitude like that, you might be one of those statistics. So, you think this is funny young man?'

After this scolding, the teacher set up the film projector. 'We are going to watch a video about the seriousness of not driving safely. Now I want you to pay attention to this film so you will not end up injured or dead because of bad decisions.'

The teacher started the film. It was titled, Red Asphalt. Some of the boys giggled about the 'fake blood' but it did seem to be graphic enough to make an imprint on some of our young minds. The teacher was trying his best to save some of our lives. The attitudes of some of the teens were already in place and they believed, 'that won't happen to me.'

Unfortunately, one of the students in the class that day was driving after drinking and the passenger was killed. There were also some of us that were seriously injured before graduation. Most of the accidents were alcohol related.

These teenage tragedies were very sad and disturbing, but for some it was no deterrent to the behaviors that are driven by our attitudes and belief systems. Some of the attitudes towards these behaviors and the beliefs attempting to explain these occurrences that I have heard are:

1. That person was just a bad driver.
2. They should know that Devils Slide is dangerous.
3. The crash wouldn't have happened if it wasn't raining.
4. That person is just accident prone.
5. They were in the wrong place at the wrong time.
6. That person has always been a loser anyway.
7. That won't happen to me.
8. They shouldn't have drunk so much.
9. They shouldn't have switched to that hard liquor.
10. That was just bad luck.

The Health Class that we took in school showed us students another educational video called, Refer Madness. I remember seeing the person in a strait jacket in a mental institution after trying some marijuana. I knew I would never try marijuana after seeing that. The film also told us that it could lead to heroin too.

When younger, I had seen the movie about a famous drummer, The Gene Krupa Story. He got hooked on marijuana and eventually lost his job with a big band and couldn't play anymore. I had also seen, The Man with the Golden Arm. A movie about a returning soldier who became a heroin addict after the war. These movies really scared me about using drugs.

I was fifteen years old in 1965. I was going to drinking parties with my friends. I was playing in a rock band in San Francisco. I didn't use drugs, but I was part of the music scene. I had learned to play the music of the Beach Boys and other surf music. I had long hair and could play any Beatle song. I was popular with the girls and having fun playing in the band. My identity crisis was over and I was enjoying life: The teenage California Dream.

One Friday night I went to a basketball game at the high school. I remember two girls from the other high school asking me if I wanted to go drink with them outside. Of course, I didn't say no. I had already been to drinking parties with my friends.

We went to the baseball field under the bleachers and the girls gave me a bottle of alcohol called 'Slow Gin.' It was dark red and tasted kinda' sweet. I had never drunk gin before. The next thing I remember was waking up in the pre-dawn, lying on the home base face down in the dirt. The girls were gone. I felt like I couldn't get up. I tried but fell back down on the ground. I knew I was going to be in trouble if I did not make it home before day-break.

Fortunately, we lived two houses from the school and I managed to basically crawl home. I made it safely into my bed before my parents awoke. What did I learn in that experiment? Don't drink 'Sloe Gin'! I also learned from drinking with my friends that if we took a little out of each bottle from our parents' different alcohols, that it not only tasted terrible, but it made us terribly sick too. What did we learn? Don't mix different types of alcohol! Our attitudes and beliefs about alcohol were being formed in our experimental stage. Hangovers were just the price you paid for the party the night before.

I mentioned we were in the middle of the 1960's. The Haight/Ashbury and Hippie culture was blooming. Our family had just moved from San Francisco to the suburbs on the peninsula. Being new to this High School, no one really knew me well. A rumor started that I was a 'nark', planted there at our school by law enforcement. I had heard one of the stoner's refer to me as "Mark the Nark'! Sure, I didn't smoke pot, and I looked like a Hippie, but it was definitely ruining my new identity as the 'cool new kid' in school.

This suspicion was not helped when I told some girlfriends mothers that they were smoking pot with a drummer from another band at school. I was just concerned about them because of my belief about marijuana at the time. After all, the Refer Madness video we saw scared me and I was afraid for their safety.

This incident caused quite a stir as the mothers called the principal and the principal called me into his office the next day. I'm quite sure the 'stoners', as we called them, were highly suspicious of me as being a 'nark'. The principal told me that there were a few suspected pot users in school and he wanted to know if I would report to him who they were. I told him I had only heard rumors and did not know for sure of anyone actually using pot.

The principal told me, "Well if you find out anything, let me know. And by the way, your hair is too long. You better get it cut shorter as I am getting complaints about how you look."

I left the principal's office. The Dean of boys was watching me leave. He had already warned me about my long hair several times. I avoided him at all cost. As I walked by him, he yelled to me, "If you don't cut your hair I will suspend you!"

It was clear that the principal and dean had an attitude towards me, and I likewise was developing an attitude toward them. I was starting to believe that they were the enemy with their threats of suspension, just because I had long hair and played in a band. I was learning to resent authority figures at that time.

I escaped from 'narkin out' on anyone. For the rest of the week I had to hide and avoid the principal and dean. I was not going to cut my hair. My attitude was; they can't tell me how to wear my hair!

School was getting stressful with the added pressure from the principal and dean. I had nightmares about these men chasing me down the halls.

Shortly after this incident, I started to feel another kind of pressure. Peer pressure. I didn't fit in with the 'jocks' because of my long hair. They had also threatened to cut my hair and kick my but too. I had so many nicknames at school, most of them very derogatory, such as; queer, faggot, girly, woos, pussy boy, and many other unmentionable nicknames. Plus, the unwanted… 'Mark the nark'. My only escape was going home after school, playing my guitar, and practicing with the band on weekends in San Francisco.

I still continued to attend drinking parties with my friends, but the stoners were staying away from me. That was OK because my attitude was that drugs were bad, and I believed that marijuana would make you insane and lead to heroin addiction.

One Friday night I attended a school dance with my three new drinking friends. We drank before we got there, just enough to get a buzz and not be obviously drunk. We had learned that if you are drunk and smell like booze, the teachers will notice. We had to be sneaky about it. We had mouthwash and gum to hide the smell, and dashes of after shave too.

During the dance, I was approached by three older girls. They wanted to know if I wanted to take a ride with them to the beach. Of course, I said yes.

They had a Volkswagen Bug. I got in the back seat with one of the girls. They parked at the beach south of San Francisco. I figured we were going down to the beach and drink alcohol.

One of the girls opened the glove box and pulled out a small box. She opened it up and grabbed a pipe out of her purse. It looked like she was putting marijuana in the pipe. They looked at me and asked, "Are you a nark?"

"No, I am not a nark!"

"If you are not Mark the nark, you can prove it by smoking this pot with us."

They handed me the pipe. I took a hit and started coughing. They laughed and took the pipe and passed it around. They were giggling and acting weird. "Are you stoned Mark?"

"Yes." I lied to them. I didn't really feel different at all. I felt a little dizziness from coughing my brains out!

"Good, now we can tell the rest of the stoners that you are OK. We got Mark the nark stoned." We all laughed. My attitude and belief about drugs and stoners changed that night. I learned that I didn't go insane from smoking marijuana, and I had fun with these 'stoner girls.'

I believed the video Refer Madness was not true. The teachers were just trying to scare us with a lie. I was learning to not believe what the teachers were teaching us about these things.

Well, word got around the school that I was now a stoner and a Hippie. My identity was getting cooler. I apologized to the girls whose mothers' I had told about their smoking marijuana. They were still upset. I definitely learned that narkin' on friends was not cool.

On the next weekend, the drummer picked me up for practice. As we cruised the Great Highway down by Ocean Beach towards San Francisco, I told the drummer, "I smoked marijuana last weekend with some girls at school."

He immediately pulled the car over and parked at Ocean Beach. He reached over and pulled a pipe out of the glove compartment. "I am so glad. Now I don't have to hide the fact that I smoke pot. Did you get stoned?"

"Not really, nothing really happened."

"Well I got the good stuff. Take a hit of this!"

We smoked and the car filled up with pot smoke as thick as fog. I was feeling very strange and disoriented. He laughed at me as I was obviously stoned.

"Now we can go to practice. The band is going to be glad that you are a stoner. They have also been hiding it from you."

When we got to practice in San Francisco, the other musicians were waiting for us.

The lead guitarist asked, "Where have you guys been, we've been waiting for you for an hour!"

The drummer pointed at me and stated, "We were at the beach getting stoned!"

I stood there in a stupor as they cheered my induction into the drug world. They immediately pulled out the pot. Playing music was never the same again. We just jammed and jammed and jammed. Music had always been my escape. Now music and pot was a total escape. My attitude about pot and drugs was changing, and I no longer believed pot was a dangerous drug. I would eventually realize that pot was a gateway drug in my life.

At this point of my life, I had never driven. The most dangerous thing I had done was walk around at night drunk. One time I fell into the Russian River after drinking too much Red Mountain Wine and almost drowned. Now I was being driven around by drivers who were under the influence.

Our attitudes and beliefs were being formed in this 'experimental stage' of use, and paved the way for our behavior and the choices we made through the rest of high school.

I had friends in school that experimented with alcohol and drugs and decided they didn't really like feeling out of control, or, they just didn't like the way it made them feel. A bad hangover or overdose was enough for certain people, and some just partied in moderation. For others, they had started in the progression of use to abuse and beyond to addiction.

The group I was with developed a lifestyle of partying. The band I played in was part of the rock music scene in San Francisco. Our first big gig was at the Fillmore Auditorium. We were going to be the opening band for a well-known group from Europe called Them, with Van Morrison. They had a big hit on the radio at the time called 'Gloria'.

This was exciting for us as an unknown garage band.

The drummer picked me up for the concert. As he drove down the coast highway, he explained to me that the whole band was going to take LSD for the gig tonight, and that they thought it would be a good idea for me to be on the 'same wave-length'. He assured me that it would be a fun experience. "Most of the Hippies at these concerts are 'trippin' on acid."

Once again, I didn't say no. We stopped at the beach and he took out some purple pills from his pocket. "Take one of these, it's Purple Haze."

I took the pill and swallowed it.

The drummer looked at me approvingly. "By the time we get to the concert, you should start feeling it."

We arrived at the Fillmore Auditorium just as the sun was setting. I noticed the bright reddish sky as we entered the building. Inside was another world. There were about 100 Hippies on the dance floor with fringe coats, and multicolored tie-dye clothes. Psychedelic projections were swirling on the walls. I followed the drummer back stage. The band was there tuning up their guitars. I put my bass case on a table and took it out to tune.

The guitarist looked at me and asked the drummer, "Did Mark take the acid?"

"Yes," replied the drummer with a funny grin. He should be coming on to it by the time we start to play."

One of the band members gave me a dark brown fringe coat to wear on stage. I was wearing bell bottoms. We looked like a Hippie rock band.

The stage manager approached us. "Are you ready to play?"

We followed him and he led us to the stage stairs.

The drummer looked at me. "Are you OK?"

"Yeh, I feel good."

I plugged in my bass and strapped it on. The announcer introduced us and the drummer counted off the first song. 1,2,3,4, take-off!

We played the first song and the audience applauded. This was so cool I couldn't believe it. We started the second song.

I was getting a strange feeling in my gut that was spreading rapidly through my body. The neck on my bass seemed to be getting longer and the strings were getting thicker. The fringes on my coat were swaying back and forth as I rocked to the music. The bell bottoms were feeling like tents drooping towards my black Beatle boots. I looked up at the melting psychedelic colored walls. I looked at the drummer and frantically asked, "What song are we playing?"

"Just keep playing!"

I somehow made it through the set. I felt like I was in an alternate universe of space and time. The crowd applauded and we left the stage. I had just been inducted into the new world of psychedelic rock.

Going back to the suburban middle class school on Monday seemed surreal. My perception of life had been radically changed. Also, my attitude toward the establishment was different. My whole belief system had been challenged.

When I look back on how I changed from being a straight, good student who thought of becoming an FBI agent, to a counter culture anti-establishment juvenile delinquent, I can understand how easy a person can get off track. The change in attitude and belief system led to a lot of choices and behaviors that had consequences in the future.

I also saw some radical changes in a few of my friends who were full of potential. Some were highly intelligent straight-A-students that, like me, barely graduated with C's or D's and just didn't care anymore. Some of us got busted for drugs as juveniles and ended up in the juvenile detention centers. Others became quickly addicted and graduated from marijuana to heroin; just like we were warned about.

I was shocked to find that there were people I knew using needles to inject heroin and speed. The experimental use progressed, for some of us, past recreational/ social use to habitual/abuse, and beyond to hardcore addiction. Our new attitude was; I'll try anything once. And if we liked it we would continue use despite negative consequences.

As a generation of baby boomers, we were being influenced by the culture of our times. Some of us had moved from the experimental stage past the social/recreational to the habitual, abuse and even addiction before we were even out of high school.

There were only a handful of addicts, but we were a growing problem in our culture. The times were changing fast.

CHAPTER 6

WHAT IS ALCOHOLISM AND ADDICTION?

I n the last class, we talked about the progression from no use to experimental use and social/recreational, and finally; abuse to addiction. In this class, we will learn the definition of alcohol/drug abuse and dependence.

We have all heard of the terms alcoholic and drug addict. Alcoholism was what alcoholics suffered from. Heroin addicts were labeled as 'junkies.' Society's views of these people were often judgmental. These were just bad people. They were called 'Low-lifers'. They hung out in dive bars and alleyways with brown paper bags of cheap wine, or with needles sticking out of their arms in cheap hotels.

I remember my father taking me down to the Tenderloin District, in San Francisco, and showing me these people when I was 13. He told me if I didn't get a good education and go to college, I might end up like these people. He said they would end up in jail, or die in an alley somewhere.

There were movies I had seen about hopeless alcoholics going insane, and heroin addicts overdosing and dying. These movies never had a very happy ending.

The medical hospitals considered alcoholics as incurable and untreatable. If they were admitted to a hospital, they were cleaned up, sobered up, and released to repeat the same hopeless pattern of behavior. They would eventually be jailed, institutionalized, or die.

In the 1930's, there were a couple of men who were considered alcoholics, and when they met, they started Alcoholics Anonymous. These men were not the alcoholics in the alleys. Bill Wilson and Doctor Bob were professional people, but were suffering the consequences of alcoholism. Bill Wilson had found a way to stop drinking by going out and helping other alcoholics to sober up and talking to them; one alcoholic to another. He told Doctor Bob who had not found a way to quit drinking about this method of helping another alcoholic to stay sober, and they started the program of Alcoholics Anonymous in 1934. This new 12-step-program gave hope to alcoholics worldwide.

Alcoholics Anonymous has an unofficial definition of an alcoholic:

'An alcoholic is a person who cannot predict with accuracy what will happen when he or she takes a drink.'

Alcoholics Anonymous also has an operative definition:

'If alcohol is causing a problem; you have a problem.'

If an alcoholic wanted help; there was finally hope and recovery from alcoholism. The only requirement for membership in Alcoholics Anonymous is a desire to quit.

In 1953, another 12-step program, Narcotics Anonymous, was co-founded by Jimmy Kinnon. It was for people with substance abuse and addiction problems in common.

Many other 12 step programs exist for addictions to gambling, sex and relationship addiction, food addiction, cocaine, nicotine and marijuana addiction. There are also programs for; Adult Children of Alcoholics; AL-Anon for friends and families of people with addiction problems; and similarly, Alateen... for teenagers affected by someone else's drinking.

These non-profit 12-step programs have helped millions of alcoholics and addicts. They have offered hope to those suffering the negative consequences of addictions, with alcoholic/addict persons helping other alcoholic/addicts. The only requirement for membership is the desire to quit and remain sober by working the 12 steps of recovery.

The disease concept of alcoholism was considered for a long time before the American Society of Addiction Medicine and the National Council on Alcoholism and Drug Dependence defined alcoholism in 1992:

'Alcoholism is a primary chronic disease with genetic, psychosocial, and environmental factors influencing its development and manifestation. The disease is often progressive and fatal. It is characterized by impaired control over drinking, preoccupation with the drug (alcohol), use of alcohol despite adverse consequences, and distortions in thinking, most notably denial. Each of these symptoms may be continuous or periodic.' (Morse, Flavin, et al., 1992)

The distinct symptoms for Alcohol Dependence were classified in the DSM-IV, which is the Diagnostic and Statistical Manual of Mental Disorders: a publication of the American Psychiatric association that classifies mental illness. Here is the section referencing Diagnostic Criteria for Substance-Use Disorders.

The Criteria for Substance Dependence

A **maladaptive pattern** of substance use, leading to clinically significant impairment or distress, as manifested by three (or more) of the following, occurring at any time in the same 12-month period:

1. **Tolerance, as defined by either of the following:**
   a) **A need for markedly increased amounts of the substance to achieve intoxication or desired effect.**
   b) **Markedly diminished effect with continued use of the same amount of the substance.**

Now to illustrate these criteria, let us say you were used to drinking two drinks, or smoking two joints to get the desired effect. Eventually you found yourself drinking three or four or five or more, and smoking as many joints to get the desired effect. This indicates that you have developed tolerance to the drug of use, and you are now increasing your use as a result. Maybe you have switched to a stronger alcoholic beverage or more potent drug. If this has occurred in the last year, you would answer yes to these criteria.

2. **Withdrawal, as manifested by either of the following:**
   a) **The characteristic withdrawal syndrome for the substance.**
   b) **The same (or a closely related) substance is taken to relieve or avoid withdrawal symptoms.**

We have all heard about withdrawals from heavy drugs like heroine and alcohol. I ask people in these classes if they have ever been through withdrawal. There are usually a few people who have been to a detox clinic to manage withdrawal symptoms from hard drugs or alcohol. Now let's say you are a coffee drinker. What happens if you do not get your coffee in the morning? Because caffeine is a central nervous system stimulant, and a psychoactive drug, you may find it hard to get going. You probably have a headache behind the eyes and the front of your head. You may become very irritable. Have you ever heard someone say, 'don't talk to me, I haven't had my coffee yet.' Because caffeine is addictive, it is listed in the new DSM-V. Energy drinks and coffee make caffeine one of the most used addictive drugs, and has many uncomfortable withdrawal symptoms.

Many of our cigarette smokers know that nicotine is highly addictive. When you are close to running out of cigarettes, you immediately start thinking about getting a new supply. The thought of running out and going through withdrawals from nicotine is not what you desire. Some people who quit smoking can become quite irritable during this process.

When I was a cigarette smoker, we used to take a break halfway through these classes. I would watch the time so I could take that much-needed cigarette break. Now when I quit, I noticed that I wasn't watching the time to take care of my nicotine addiction. The smokers in the class would start getting their cigarettes and lighters out and start fidgeting in their seats. If I wasn't paying attention, they would start pointing at the clock. Many smokers start withdrawal symptoms and can get quite uncomfortable if not allowed a cigarette break.

Drinkers who are addicted, might need a drink in the morning because they have the shakes, and must drink to steady their nerves. Heavy drinkers may refer to, 'the hair of the dog that bit you', or a 'Bloody Mary' or 'Smoza' in the morning to relieve a hangover. The symptoms of withdrawal occur with any drug of which a person has developed dependence.

So, if any of these criteria have happened to you in the last year, you would answer yes.

3. The substance is often taken in larger amounts or over a longer period than was intended.

An example of this might be someone who has had problems leaving a drinking establishment after 'happy hour.' Maybe 'happy hour' has turned into 'happy hours.' Perhaps this has caused problems in family relationships or other areas of life. This person might be trying to stop this problematic behavior… and tries to stay away from the social 'happy hour'.

Now say this person is getting ready to leave work, and his co-workers invite him to 'happy hour' to watch the playoffs at a sports bar. He is trying to be good so says, "No thanks, I have to be somewhere a little later." The co-worker might say, "Oh come on over for a little while, everybody is going to be there."

This peer pressure is enough to get him over there. On the way, he is telling himself he will just have a drink or two and just stay for one hour. That's the plan.

He gets to the bar with his friends and orders a drink. When he finishes the drink, he looks at his watch and sees he has time for one more. Ok, no problem, one more. He finishes that drink and gets up to go. He must follow his plan so he can make it to his commitment with the family at 6:30. His friend offers to buy him a drink, so he agrees and sits back down. He drinks it fast so he can get out of there and as he gets near the exit, an old friend arrives and is excited to see him.

"Where are you going? Let me buy you a drink. Come on, you've got time to have a drink with an old buddy."

He puts his arm around his shoulder and guides him toward the bar. Another drink and the fun is starting, and then someone buys a round for everyone at the bar. Another drink! After that drink, he looks at his watch and he is late for that family commitment. He is starting to think through the 'alcohol influenced' brain, and might say to himself that he is already in trouble… so he may as well stay and have some more fun.

The 'happy hours' have passed and the next thing he knows, he hears the bartender say, "Last call!" He realizes he has done it again. He drank more than he planned and stayed longer than he intended.

If this has been happening to you in the last year, you would answer yes to these criteria. This can also apply to people that don't drink and just use other drugs. Maybe they were just going to a friend's house to smoke a joint and ended up partying a lot longer when someone with some cocaine showed up. The party could go on late into the night before you know it. With the upper drug methamphetamine, all night into the next day!

4. There is a persistent desire or unsuccessful efforts to cut down or control substance use.

Most problem drinkers or drug users have attempted to cut down or control substance use. They really don't want to quit completely. They might attempt to go back to drinking just two drinks a day, or just partying on weekends. They don't want to admit that they are out of control; they can cut down and get control again. Most alcoholics and addicts have probably attempted this many times, but were unsuccessful. If this has happened in the past year, your answer would be yes to these criteria.

5. A great deal of time is spent in activities necessary to obtain the substance (E.G., visiting multiple doctors or driving long distances), use the substance (E.G., chain smoking), or recover from its effects.

When there weren't any all-night stores close by, people would drive long distances to the liquor store. In the urban areas, people would have to drive many miles to the nearest town to get more alcohol. If the drug you want is illegal, you might have to go to find drugs in the streets, or wait for some dealer to go get it. More time is usually spent getting drugs in the 'black market.'

So, you then spend a great deal of time using your drug or drugs of choice. Maybe the whole weekend is spent in these activities? Missing work on Mondays because of being the so called 'week-end warrior' might be a pattern that develops, as it takes more time to recover from the effects of using. Weekends might start on Friday and last all weekend or longer.

If these things are happening to you in the last year, yes would be the answer to these criteria.

6. Important social, occupational, or recreational activities are given up or reduced because of substance use.

Some examples of these activities might be; if you were involved in social events where there is no drinking or drug use. Maybe school PTA or religious meetings would be avoided. Work activities might be given up if you were under the influence and getting drug tested is a possibility. If you are involved in sports activities, alcohol or other drug use might be inappropriate for participating in these activities, and therefore avoided.

If any of these types of situations have happened to you in the past year, you would answer yes to these criteria.

7. Drinking or using continues even when it is known that physical or psychological problems are caused by or aggravated by continued use.

I have seen people continue to drink even though they had been diagnosed with cirrhosis of the liver, and if they did not stop they would get worse and probably die. There have been people that contracted Hepatitis C and continued drug use even though it would make their condition worse, even to the result of death. Many people, who were using drugs via intravenous injection, were sharing dirty needles and therefore contracting the human immunodeficiency virus (HIV) which can develop into acquired immune deficiency syndrome (AIDS). Many addicts were not aware of this risk, and some who were aware were willing to take that risk in order to use the drug or drugs of choice.

People who suffer from psychological problems, often self-medicate, which can worsen their problems immensely. Drinking and using drugs can interfere with psychiatric drugs that are prescribed for mental disorders, therefore disrupting the effectiveness of the prescribed drugs.

Using despite negative consequences in any of these criteria would mean a yes answer in this category.

So if you answered yes, that three or more of these seven items occur in the same 12-month period, you could be diagnosed as having an Alcohol/Drug Dependence Disorder.

If you did not meet the criteria for dependence, the DSM also has criteria for alcohol or other drug abuse. We will now look at the criteria for Alcohol/Drug Abuse.

DSM-IV Criteria for Alcohol or Drug Abuse

The DSM-IV describes alcohol, and or drug abuse as: A **maladaptive pattern** of use leading to clinically significant impairment or distress, when one (or more) of the following have occurred in a 12-month period.

1. **Recurrent drinking or using that results in a failure to fulfill major obligations at work, school, or home.**

Now if you have been missing work on Mondays which establishes a pattern, your boss or co-workers might notice this pattern. Maybe you are too hung over from partying on the weekend to make it to work on Monday, and when you do make it to work you are not quite capable of doing a good job.

At school, you might be missing classes, getting behind on homework, and your grades might be dropping because of poor performance due to alcohol or drug use.

At home, you might be absent from important obligations concerning the family due to alcohol or drug use. Maybe you missed a birthday or other important family event caused by your alcohol or drug activities.

2. **Recurrent drinking or using when it is physically hazardous, such as while driving, or when involved in any risky recreational activities.**

It is possible that the people in a DUI program would not answer yes to these criteria. The word recurrent is defined as: Occurring or appearing again or repeatedly. Some people may have only driven once and received a DUI. Among the thousands of DUI participants whom I have counseled, it is very rare. Most people have driven many times under the influence before they got arrested; some hundreds of times or more! There are many recreational activities that are risky when sober; let alone being impaired by substance use. The majority of people in the DUI program would probably answer yes in this category.

3. **Recurrent alcohol/drug related legal problems.**

With this question, this might be the first time you have ever had an arrest. Some people have never even had a traffic ticket before they were arrested for DUI. If you are here for a second DUI, or if you also have been arrested for substance-related disorderly conduct, or possession of illegal drugs, you would answer yes to this question.

4. **Continued drinking/using despite persistent or recurrent social or interpersonal problems caused or aggravated by use.**

Maybe you have had arguments with significant others or your spouse concerning consequences of being under the influence. You may have had physical fights or domestic violence occurring as a result of being under the influence. If these types of problems have been recurrent, and yet you continued drinking/using, you would answer yes to these criteria.

As you can see, an abuse disorder can be diagnosed by answering yes to only one (or more) of these four criteria. Most people may be surprised to find that they may have symptoms of an alcohol or substance abuse disorder.

There are many people who will realize that alcohol/drug use is causing problems for them. The DUI program may bring enough of a self-realization for people to stop the pattern of abuse which can lead to addiction. Then again, our Multiple Offender Program is full of people who continue to use despite the negative consequences that result from their pattern of behavior.

CHAPTER 7
GENETIC AND ENVIRONMENT RISK FACTORS

There are many theories of addiction and its causes. Some studies show that alcoholism may be an inherited trait. It might be that if you have a family history of alcoholism, you could have a higher risk for such tendencies. Intake counselors usually ask about family history of alcoholism, just as a doctor asks about family history of other diseases such as; diabetes, heart disease, cancer, and other possible hereditary tendencies.

Genetic studies find genes in the DNA that might contribute to alcohol/drug problems. DNA determines so much of who we are besides our body type, and the color of our hair and eyes. There could be a hereditary genetic predisposition that may put people at a higher risk for abuse/dependence.

Environment can also be a risk factor of abuse/dependence. Stress is a major factor which may make people susceptible to compulsive alcohol/drug use. If a child grows up in a using-culture where alcohol or other drug use is prevalent and considered normal, that child might also have a high risk of learning those behaviors and perpetuating the pattern of abuse/dependence. Children learn behaviors from family and friends that become role models for dysfunctional behavior.

If a person has a hereditary/genetic predisposition and environmental risk factors, there is probably a 'high risk' for this person. Education and awareness could be a preventative measure for 'high risk' individuals.

Addiction has been referred to as a 'family disease'. If a family exists with an alcoholic/addict, the whole family can be affected. There might be neglect, and or abuse. The abuse could be physical, emotional or psychological.

Certain roles have been identified in dysfunctional family systems. There might be one or more dependent persons. It is sometimes both parents that are involved in alcohol/drug abuse, further compounding the issues of dysfunctionality. One of the parents, who is dealing with a dependent spouse, might be playing an **'enabler'** role, often allowing the abuse to continue. Denial of the problem can also be a common trait.

Another role of family members may also be the **'family hero'**. This person might be one of the older children who are assuming the role of responsibility of being more like a parent in the family. There could also be the role of the **'scapegoat'**. This person might be blamed for many of the problems the family is having, shifting the focus from other problematic family members, as part of the denial. This person could also be at 'high risk' for use of alcohol/drugs.

Some children become what are called the **'lost child'**. This child is often passive and withdrawn. When the family is in high drama, this child would probably escape and be distant, if possible. Another child might become the **'mascot'**. This child often uses humor to get attention, or clown around to provide distraction from the seriousness of the problems in the family.

These roles have been identified as ways people in 'dysfunctional families' cope. The family system usually is dealing with a lot of pain, anger, hurt, rage, fear and guilt. Complex issues exist in these families, putting members at risk for many serious problems.

In chemically dependent families, the ideal solution would be treatment for the whole family. Often the alcoholic/addict is arrested and forced into treatment for chemical dependence. Many treatment modalities include treatment for other family members. There are programs for children, teenagers and adults of these dysfunctional families, to deal with many of the problems caused by alcohol and other drug dependence.

Professional help is often mandated when the courts and Child Protection Services are involved. Probation might require a drug treatment program for the rehabilitation of addicted persons. Child Protection Services can provide help for children whose parents are in custody.

There are also 12-step programs for teenagers such as Alateen, and Codependency groups like Al-Anon for the enabler and codependent people involved with the dependent persons. Adult Children of Alcoholics and many more self-help programs are available as support groups. Education and awareness of the causes and problems of alcohol/drug abuse are necessary to prevent risk.

Help is necessary for the whole family that is suffering from the 'family disease' of addiction. Until an intervention of the pattern of dysfunction is made, the pattern could be passed on from generation to generation.

Often the intervention is the result of legal problems such as arrest and incarceration. The children are often removed from the family by Child Protection Services. I have had clients who are going to drug programs and parenting classes in order to get their children back. They might also be required to attend 12-step programs as well. There are many mandates from the courts for these services and regular drug testing is required. It is not easy for most people to deal with all the problems that have resulted from alcohol/drug dependence. Without help to break the cycle of dysfunction, it can be overwhelming and often results in relapse into the old behaviors that have caused all the negative consequences.

We may have the goal of not driving under the influence, or maybe the goal is to stop being under the influence at all. Whatever our goals are, the stages of change can help us achieve them.

Changing risky behavior is the key to avoiding another DUI. We need to examine how to change and eliminate the 'risk factors'. Hopefully, there is the motivation to change.

The stage of not changing is called **Pre-contemplation**. They are not even contemplating change. They might be thinking that this DUI was just bad luck, and probably will not happen again, or they will just be more careful in the future. Because quitting these behaviors is not even considered… they remain at risk for another DUI, or worse.

Our goal is to move people from **Pre-contemplation** to the **Contemplation** stage. This stage is where they are considering making some changes in behaviors. Next, they will move to the **Action** stage, where they begin to change behaviors. Maybe when they drink they will stay home, or if they do go out, they will use a designated driver or call a cab. They could also be considering cutting down, or quitting altogether. Being aware of their 'risk factors' can help to change their lives for the better. By maintaining a healthy lifestyle, they can eliminate many negative consequences that may impact them in the future.

CHAPTER 8
ALCOHOL EFFECTS ON BODY, BRAIN, AND BEHAVIOR

Alcohol, when used in low-dose moderation, has been reported to have some beneficial health benefits. Moderation for women is usually defined as one drink per day; and for men two drinks per day. But for people who are at risk of addiction, or with mental health or physical problems (including pregnant women), alcohol can cause serious problems.

Alcohol affects every organ in the body. We have heard of the acute and chronic effects of alcohol with cirrhosis of the liver, but fatty liver and alcohol hepatitis can also develop. Alcohol can damage all organs of the body. It can cause damage to the gastrointestinal tract including; inflammation, pancreatitis and cancer. It can cause bleeding and inflammation in the stomach and intestines. Also, the immune system may have been in lowered resistance to disease.

The heart problems from heavy alcohol abuse are; high blood pressure, irregular heartbeat, and stroke, among other conditions.

Women are more adversely affected by alcohol than men. Besides having higher blood alcohol levels than men with equal doses, women also are more likely to develop liver damage, anemia and hypertension from lesser amounts of alcohol. Reproductive systems of women can be affected with irregular menstrual cycles and reduced chances for conception. For men, impotence may occur and testicles may atrophy.

One of the worst consequences of alcohol abuse is the increased risk of women bearing children with birth defects. The leading cause of mental retardation is Fetal Alcohol Syndrome. These babies are born with abnormal features of head and face, such as shortened eye openings, flattened midface and cleft lip and palate. They may also have heart and limb problems, retarded growth and smaller brains. Body organs can also be malformed. When these children get older they might exhibit behavioral problems. Fetal Alcohol Effects (FAE), which is a milder form of FAS, may also result from alcohol use during pregnancy. Since the 1980's, the federal government has advised pregnant women to remain abstinent to reduce risk of Fetal Alcohol Syndrome (FAS) and Fetal Alcohol Effects (FAE).

Because one drink affects the frontal cortex of the brain first, the ability to drive safely is affected. Alcohol consumption causes a sedative effect which makes the person feel relaxed with a slower reaction speed and some motor impairment. They might feel they are in control, but if they need to react to avoid an unsafe driving situation, they might not have the normal reflex action to be safe.

One to two drinks can also lower inhibitions and impair a person's judgement. Their self-confidence might be raised and they might try a maneuver beyond their ability. Increased sociability and possible sexual desire might also cause problems they normally would not initiate. When we have our class on HIV/AIDS and sexually transmitted diseases, people typically ask why we study these in a DUI class. The answer is that the risk factors for 'risky behaviors', such as unsafe sex, increase with alcohol and other drug use.

So, say you are drinking somewhere and you have one drink and feel fine. You know that you plan on driving after your done, and since you feel OK... you decide to have one more. You are using your part of the brain that is affected with just one drink, so you might be already thinking with an impaired brain. Your reasoning is that you can have another drink. Maybe your calculating what you learned about alcohol and body weight in relation to blood alcohol levels on the chart the Department of Motor Vehicles sent you with your license. Now because your memory in this part of the brain might be slightly impaired, you might not remember exactly all the variables that can be part of your blood alcohol level. And, because your caution cognition in this part of the brain is also affected, you might just go ahead and have one more drink. We might call this 'drinking thinking.'

As this happy hour passes, you are now using the command center of your brain, which is now under the influence of two drinks. If you drive now, you could be at risk for a DUI, or a Wet/Reckless. You are also more likely to have an accident. We have many people getting DUI's with just two drinks. Again, because you are feeling good and decide to drive, thinking you should be OK... you are risking a DUI!

Now, say you decide to stay. Your thinking that if you just slow down your drinking, you will be good to go later. Just one more drink starts to affect the parietal lobe of the brain, where your self-control and judgement are really affected.

Then, you might decide to go ahead and just drive. Now when you get to your car, you might do a reality check and sit in the car for a moment. You don't feel too drunk to drive, and your self-judgement tells you go ahead... you can do this. If a cop pulls you over, his judgements of you are different than yours. He will testify in court and a Judge will judge if you were under the influence while driving. Most people in the DUI program had three or four drinks when pulled over. Again, your 'drinking thinking', or impaired ability to make a good decision, have caused you to be at risk for negative consequences.

Some people may not even go through this process of even thinking about possible negative consequences, such as a DUI. Many people who have never had a DUI, may not even consider that there might be a problem.

Consider that if even one drink can affect your ability to drive safely; two or more really make you an unsafe driver. Your reaction time is slower and motor skills are impaired. If an incidence occurs where you need alertness, such as a child running into the street after a ball, you might not be able to avoid hitting the child or another pedestrian in the road. Whether you are above the legal limit or not, you are driving with impaired driving skills.

When your blood alcohol level gets to the double-digit level, .10 to .14, you are clearly not able to function normally and are a very dangerous driver. Your driving skills are seriously impaired. Three to four drinks will put most people into this level of BAC.

The next part of the brain affected with five to six drinks is the occipital lobe, where the senses are mostly located. When driving with a serious impairment of vision and coordination, you are an extremely dangerous driver. That is why the 'Extreme DUI" was lowered from .20 BAC to .15. At these levels, drivers are 25 times more likely to have a fatal accident. At the old extreme DUI level of .20, you are 100 times more likely to have a fatal accident. You are severely impaired at these levels. Blackouts and amnesia may occur. Some people don't remember driving! You might be unable to walk or stand. Coordination and balance are severely impaired.

Blood alcohol levels of .30 will cause most people to lose consciousness. At .45, most people will die from alcohol overdose. The vital centers of the brain are affected, which can cause death.

Pedestrians walking about inebriated, are also at high risk for accidents. They also become vulnerable to attack from violent predators. It is very unsafe to be in public places when drunk and high to the point where you are unaware of your surroundings. I have known people who were hit by cars, beaten up, and sexually assaulted when leaving parties or clubs alone when drunk. It is a good idea to keep an eye out for friends who are out of control. They could be at risk of endangerment to self and others.

There are some people who have a radical change in personality when drinking alcohol. We probably all know of a person who is normally very nice when sober, and then when they drink they become obnoxious, belligerent and sometimes violent. The jails and prisons are full of people who did violent crimes while under the influence.

I had a personal experience where I had this affect. It was my friend Big Mikey's 40th birthday. Four of us went out to a Denny's, where my sister was a bartender, to celebrate. We ordered quite a few rounds and were having fun. Big Mikey and I were heavy drinkers and this night… we were definitely pounding them down.

I was keeping an eye on my younger sister the bartender, as there was a rowdy guy at the bar. He wasn't hurting anyone but was a very obnoxious drunk. There was a huge guy standing at the end of the bar. He walked over to the much smaller rowdy guy at the bar who was mouthing off to other customers. The big man grabbed the smaller guy by the throat and told him if he didn't shut up he was going to take him out to the parking lot and beat the crap out of him.

Now I didn't know either one of these guys, but being a smaller person myself, I don't like to see bigger guys bullying people smaller than themselves, so I got I little 'bent out of shape' and told my friends that I was going to go over and set things straight with that big bully. My friends tried to talk me out of going over there, but I said I needed to teach that 'bully' a lesson.

Meanwhile, the big guy went over to his table with three other huge guys and sat down. My sister was talking to the obnoxious drunk on the bar stool. I got up and slowly walked over to the table with the big guys. I had plenty of 'liquid courage in me.' The huge guy looked at me as I stood there at the end of their table with a confused look on his face. I put my hand out to shake his hand. He put down his drink and shook my hand. I told him my sister was the bartender and that I did not like him bullying the guy at the bar. I said that if he wanted to pick on a small guy he could meet me in the parking lot. His friends and my friends were all watching me intently. I let go of his hand and slowly walked back to my table. Big Mikey shook his head and told me that I was crazy. My other friends agreed. They decided I shouldn't drink anymore.

The huge guy from the other table walked back up to the bar and was talking to my sister. After he left, I went to the bar to see if my sister was alright. I asked her what the big guy said to her. She told me that he was her bouncer and he asked her if she wanted him to throw me out of the bar. She told him that I was her older brother and that sometimes when I drink I can be very crazy and dangerous. She told him to just let me alone and that my friends would take care of me.

I asked her for another drink and she told me no. I don't remember much after that.

I saw the same big bouncer years later after I had gotten sober. I went over to make amends to him for that night. He told me it was OK and that my sister told him she has two brothers that nobody wants to mess with when they are drunk because they are crazy. I just laughed and looked at him with disbelief. He probably could have kicked my butt when I was drunk. Maybe even when I was sober!

I used to think that my behavior was caused by the fact that I was Irish, Scotch and Cherokee Indian. When those three would get too drunk, they would go on the war-path together and raise a little hell. I was 'Running with the Devil!'

CHAPTER 9
CHANGING ATTITUDES, BELIEFS AND CHOICES

Attitudes and beliefs are part of the decision-making process which may influence our choices that determine our paths in life. In this class, we will learn our new ABC's. *A* stands for attitude; *B* is for beliefs; *C* is for choices. Let us start with the definition of attitude.

There are at least 7 categories of attitude in the Webster's dictionary. One is; a position or bearing as indicating for the action, feeling or mood; the feeling or mood itself. Another; a behavior representative of feeling or conviction; a disposition that is primarily grounded in affect and emotion and is expressive of opinions rather than belief; an organismic state of readiness to act that is often accompanied by considerable affect and that may be activated by an appropriate stimulus into significant or meaningful behavior. And the final definition: a persistent disposition either positive or negative toward a person, group, object, or value.

Now most of us are familiar with persons being described as having either a 'bad attitude', or a 'good attitude'. We have also heard of 'negative or positive' attitudes.

Society also has attitudes that change over time. The attitude 50 years ago, about 'drunk driving' was quite different than these days. Some of you that are older people might remember when a cop would pull you over and instead of arresting you, they would offer options. If you weren't that drunk, they might give you a warning and tell you to be careful. If you had an open container and were drinking while driving, they would sometimes just empty out the open container into the street and tell you they are doing you a favor, and then let you go.

If you were definitely inebriated, they might have the passenger with you drive if they were in better shape than you.

I am a recovering drunk driver. I remember when I was pulled over after leaving a bar after two-o'clock. It was one of those nights when the people in the bar where we were playing music, bought the band many drinks. Every time we played the song Free Bird, we would get 'free drinks'. That night we had too many free drinks.

When I left the bar, I was driving two of the musicians' home, who happened to be blind. I was driving down the coast highway when I noticed I needed gas, so I made a U turn at the intersection to drive into a gas station. A police car followed me and parked behind me as I got out to pump gas. It was the 1970's and it was the first female cop I had ever seen. She got out of her car and approached me carefully. She asked me if I had been drinking. I told her the usual answer that I had a couple of beers during the night. We knew that if we lied to the cops and said we hadn't been drinking, they would know we were lying and might be tougher on us.

She asked me if I could walk a straight line for her. I decided to show off my skills and walked the yellow line by the gas pump, doing a hand stand. Coins fell from my pockets and were rolling around the lot. I stood up and smiled at her. She just shook her head and asked me if anyone in the car could drive. I told her that they were both blind.

She walked over to the car and approached the passenger, who was the blind drummer for the band. He had a long beard and long hair and did not wear sun glasses like most blind people wore. She asked him for his driver's license and shined the light into his eyes, which were missing the pupils. He covered his eyes with his long fingers and told her the light hurt his eyes. She then asked the rear seat passenger for her license. She told her she doesn't have one as she is legally blind.

The lady cop returned to me standing near the pumps. She asked me if I could call someone to come drive us home. I told her I didn't know anyone to call. She told me that she would follow me as I drove them home. She did follow me, and when I dropped the lady singer at home, the cop asked me where I had to go to take the other person home. I told her San Francisco.

She followed me to the town border and then turned around and drove back down the coastal town we had just left. The drummer asked me, "Did she go back?"

"Yes, she has gone."

"Oh good, now can I fire up this joint?"

"Go ahead, the coast is clear!"

So, we smoked a joint on the way back to San Francisco. Now when I look back on that time, I would have definitely been arrested for drunk driving. And to think how drunk I was and that the police officer let me go! I was clearly a danger to society, and still I continued to drive home after gigs quite inebriated. I was pulled over many times in the 1970's and not arrested.

Another time the police told me to pull over off the road and sleep it off, and they would come back later to check on me. Nowadays people get a DUI sleeping it off in their car.

In the 1980's a police officer offered to drive me home because I was really wasted. Those things do not happen anymore.

Now the only ride they give you is to jail. Law enforcements attitude about drunk drivers has really changed over last few decades. They no longer offer the options they used to.

Law enforcement officers also receive DUI's now. I have had many sheriffs, police officers and Highway Patrol officers in these classes in the last decade. Newspaper headlines frequently highlight these arrests. Most arrests are likely in the back pages under police activities. Occasionally an officer will give a fellow officer a break, and when the newspapers find out an investigation is launched with much media coverage. Once pulled over, hardly anybody gets away with a DUI anymore.

Society has had a change in attitude concerning Driving Under the Influence. Media coverage of 'horrific' DUI accidents like the one back on May 14, 1988, when a drunken motorist crashed into a school bus killing 27 people, is an example of media helping change societies attitude.

The *'War on Drunk Driving'* is a nationwide program. Legislation of tougher DUI laws are being passed as the public awareness of the DUI problem is highlighted. The DUI arrests for females, and especially among young women, has increased dramatically. Many people with 3,4,5 and more DUI's are still driving. Some cities have DUI task forces and teams to track down repeat offenders who fail to appear in the courts or are on the run to avoid their sentences. There is an increase in Sobriety Checkpoints as part of the 'crackdown' on impaired drivers. Our society no longer believes Driving Under the Influence is acceptable. The 'Zero Tolerance' for DUI is the result of the growing awareness of society about this major safety problem.

Society's change in attitudes and beliefs has been instrumental in changing the way we think about Driving Under the Influence. We as individuals need to change our attitudes and beliefs so we can think through the choices we make that affect the safety of our communities.

CHAPTER 10

THE LAST CLASS: MADD IMPACT PANEL

I was sitting in my office preparing for the last lesson in the DUI education class. For eight years, I had been teaching classes and leading process groups. This was my final day. I was looking at the empty walls of the office that yesterday were decorated with my favorite pictures; they seemed so bare! The only one left was the poster of 44 men, women and children who died on one typical day on the roads as victims of DUI related accidents: Faces given to the numerical statistics. There were also the framed certifications: Anger Management, Domestic Violence, Dual Diagnosis and Alcohol and Other Drugs College Graduation Certification-1999. It had been 14 years since I had begun this counseling journey!

I looked out from the third-floor window overlooking the city of trees. I breathed deeply, meditated and prayed for my last chance to reach the 30 DUI clients I knew that were waiting in the classroom. This was my regular routine of preparing for groups; when time permitted.

Leaving the office, I could hear the familiar sound of clients down the hall in the classroom. I entered the class and looked at the mix of people; ages 18 to 78. The full spectrum of society was sitting before me. There were young people still in high school, college students and teachers. Professional people: Doctors, nurses, lawyers, veterans, business persons, housewives, divorcees, singles, and even law enforcement. Also, people of every race, religion, and ethnicity living in a melting pot city. And all with one thing in common: They were in the criminal justice system for driving under the influence.

I greeted the class and introduced myself to the new clients. I then did role call from the roster to make sure all present had signed in and that all who signed in were present. Occasionally a client would sign in and leave, thinking they might not be noticed!

I erased the whiteboard of the previous day's lesson and wrote today's topic on the board with thick black erasable ink.

MADD IMPACT PANEL

"Part of our new curriculum was to have speakers from Mothers Against Drunk Driving. MADD also presents DUI Impact Panels for those mandated to attend by probation. They have not sent a speaker today, so, I decided to share with you my personal experience of having lost my son to a drunken driving accident. The difference between my story and those told at MADD is that my son was not killed by a drunk driver: He was the drunk driver who died!"

I had told many stories over the years to my classes as a teaching method. Usually around Thanksgiving when my son died, I would tell the hardest story to share. My passion and emotion for this lesson were intense. The class listened intently; even the ones who would usually tune out. This was my best chance to reach the young clients that sat before me. Many of them were the same age as my son and his friends; 18 to 25-years-old. This population was at very high risk for death by DUI! I saw one young man in the back who reminded me of my own son at that age. I took a deep breath and began my story.

When I finished, I ended with stating: "My main goal of teaching is to reduce the risk of suffering the extreme negative consequences of DUI. Injuring or killing themselves or others is what I considered '*unacceptable risk.*' The fact that any of us could be at risk of being charged with manslaughter, or even murder, is a reality. I also consider myself to be at risk. I am a recovering alcoholic/addict with no guarantee of never drinking again. If I relapsed, and, with impaired judgment decided to drive under the influence, what would I risk? I could go from DUI counselor on one day, to being in court charged with DUI the next. And, if someone was injured or died… I could go to prison with the horrible realization that I had killed or injured someone! I consider this to be: Totally '*unacceptable risk*'."

I started to erase the whiteboard. "Some of you are completing your DUI education tonight. Let us review some of the things you have learned that are useful to you."

We finished the review. As the students left the classroom, a couple of people approached me to talk. A couple thanked me for the information saying they learned a lot and would not be the ones who would ever be back. I always hoped that was true for them. Reducing recidivism, for getting arrested for another DUI, is a main goal of the DUI School.

A middle-aged woman was the last one in the room with me. She spoke to me very seriously. "As a mother arrested for drunk driving, I am ashamed that I may have risked injury or death to someone because of being impaired. I cannot imagine losing a child. Thank you so much for sharing your story. I know it must be hard for you to revisit that tragedy your family experienced. I am completing your class today and have learned so much. I love all the stories you tell to teach these valuable lessons. Why don't you put them all in a book? I wish I would have known all of this before

I decided to drink and drive. If you wrote about it, I would give it to all my friends to read. I am thankful that I heard your final story of how DUI has impacted you personally."

She shook my hand. Her eyes were rimmed with tears. She left me alone in the classroom. I looked around the room in which I had spent the last seven years teaching thousands of DUI clients. I closed the door and walked down the hall to my office. I sat in the chair and looked out the window with a heavy heart.

The phone display was blinking, indicating a new message. After a minute of silent meditation, I listened to the message.

"Hi Mark, Wendy here. I am calling you to let you know that Pastor Chuck has passed away and the memorial is this Saturday. If you want to go with me, give me a call!"

Pastor Chuck was a counselor at Free at Last and other clinics in the Bay Area. He also was part of the Music Matters Ministry. I used to teach HIV-AIDS classes in San Francisco with Pastor Chuck for drug offenders.

I picked up the phone and called Wendy to arrange going to the Bay Area to attend the memorial service with her.

"Hi Wendy."

"Mark! Oh my gosh, I am so glad you called. Do you want to go with me to Pastor Chuck's memorial?"

"Sure, when is it?"

"It's next Saturday at 11:00 in Palo Alto. Come down to my house at about 10:00 and we can go together."

"OK, I'll see you Saturday at 10:00 then."

"I am so glad you are going with me! I'll see you Saturday morning."

Wendy has been my long-time friend since the 1960's. When I left my Mother's house at the age of seventeen, I spent some time on Wendy's couch. She was the "Hippy" Mother who let our rock bands practice in her living room. Wendy was "hipper than hip!"

I was very blessed to have her in my life at this time; and all those decades since the sixties.

Wendy and I had lived through the middle of the psychedelic era, hangin' out in the Haight Ashbury and the San Francisco 'rock scene!'

Thirty years later, in the mid 1990's, we both got clean and sober and changed our lives through recovery. I took her to an A.A. meeting I had been attending for about a year when she reached her bottom. Wendy was soon working the steps in the Big Book with a sponsor. We were in recovery together.

One Friday night, we went to a Higher Power meeting in the Bay Area. Pastor Chuck and the Music Matters Ministry band were playing that night. We became regulars at that meeting for years, introducing "newcomers" to the Higher Power. Pastor Chuck had a powerful message through his music. It was a joyful event and was instrumental in changing many lives in the local recovery community.

I drove to the Bay Area early Saturday morning. The smell of the sea salt air triggered memories. The view from the bridge of the city brought back the past; flooding my brain like a down pouring rain. I wanted to stop in San Francisco but I just kept going. I would stop there on my way back.

Millions of thoughts marauded through my mind. Every exit off the freeway going south was a stimulus of stories from my past. They would fast forward and blur by into the next city town. I continued past the San Francisco airport to the Port of Redwood City; a route I drove thousands of times as a Yellow Cab driver after getting sober. More 'cabbie' stories!

I took the turnoff to Wendy's and arrived on time. She answered the door. "Come in Mark, I'm almost ready. Have a seat."

"No thanks, my butt is sore from the two-hour drive down here."

"Help yourself to some sodas in the fridge."

I looked at all the pictures on her fridge. Her little children I used to babysit, now had their own little children. Some were not so little, in fact, adults now. The next generation!

"Did you see my granddaughter?"

"Yes, I can't believe you're a Grandmother!"

"OK, I'm ready… Let's hit the road."

We continued our journey as we caught up on our lives.

The memorial was at a church in Palo Alto. We arrived in time and entered the sanctuary. There were hundreds of people in attendance for his memorial. His surviving brothers gathered on the stage and began to sing. The Music Matters Ministry was still alive in song. His message lives on, though he has passed on. I remember the first time I heard them sing, and the joy to my spirit the music could bring. It was a grand celebration of a life that had been recovered to help others.

We visited afterwards… with people we had not seen in years. Death often brings people together. Pastor Chuck's life was a testament to faith.

After saying goodbye to his widow, we walked through the parking lot to the car. I realized that we were in the same area that my son had been buried. I had thought about visiting my son's grave for years.

"Wendy, do you have time to go to the cemetery where my son was buried?"

"Why sure Mark, do you know how to get there?"

"I will have to look it up on my map. I know it is up on the western hillside of this town."

I pulled out the map and searched for cemeteries. It had been long time since I had been there. I found it on the map.

"OK, I know where it is."

We soon found the cemetery where he was buried. Driving through the old ivy covered gates, we followed the road surrounded by headstones to the main office. I slowly exited the car and stretched, inhaling the flower fragrant air into my lungs. My friend Wendy sitting in the passenger seat looked at me with a worried look on her caring face.

"So, you want me to go in there with you?"

"No, that's alright… thanks. I'll just go in and get the directions to the gravesite."

"OK, I'll just wait for you."

She looked at me, with her compassionate "counselor" eyes, as I walked toward the cemetery office.

A cherub looking lady with big brown eyes, sat in the office behind the desk.

"May I help you sir?"

"Why yes. I am here to visit my son's grave."

"And what was your son's name?"

"David Burton."

She typed the name into the computer.

"That would be in section six, plot 23, on Miranda Circle. Do you know where that is located?"

"No. It has been a long time since I was last here."

"O.K. Let me get you a map and highlight where it is."

She pulled out the yellow highlighter. "We are right here. Follow the road in front down two streets, and make a right. The next left will be Magnolia Circle. Does he have a headstone?"

"I'm not sure, I think so."

"Let me get the grounds keeper to show you where it is. If you get lost, we close in fifteen minutes and won't be here to help you find his grave site."

"Yes, that would be great. Thank you so much."

She paged the person to come to the office. I looked at the serene pictures of waterfalls in the woods, and another with a dirt path along a cliff by the ocean. There was a room for families to meet, and a prayer room with stained glass.

A tall, well-dressed man appeared seemingly from nowhere, as my attention was lost in space and time.

"Do you need help to find a grave site?"

"Yes, I do."

"Follow me."

He walked to the door and opened it for me. We walked to the car and I lowered myself into the driver's seat.

"I have the map. We can follow that man and he will show us the site, so we don't get lost."

"Oh good."

I gave Wendy the map. The man stood next to the car and looked down at me. "I'll walk straight across that hill and you can drive with your friend around that bend to the dead-end circle."

I started the car as he headed over the hill. I looked at Wendy. "Interesting choice of words. Cul-de-sac would have been a good euphemism for dead-end."

We followed the map and drove around the hill to Magnolia Circle where the man was waiting. I parked the car and Wendy asked me, "Do you want me to go with you for this?"

"You don't have to. I think I will be alright."

"Are you sure?"

"I will be right back."

"OK, I'm here if you need me."

"I better go before I lose my guide."

I walked up the slow sloping hill, trying not to step on any grave sites. The man was searching the area of flat headstones decorated with vases of old and fading flowers. There were also odd looking ornaments and various religious symbols on some of the grave sites. As he knelt down and brushed away some overgrown grass on one of the flat headstones, the name was revealed: David Burton.

"Yes, that is the one."

As he continued to clean the stone, the dates with the dash between them were legible; **1969-1991**. There written in stone; the sad reality at my feet. Our lives ultimately start with a date and a dash followed by another date; the end! What happens during that dash is our lifetime line. For some, it's a fifty-yard dash, or, maybe one hundred. For others, it may be a couple of laps. Then there are those doing the marathon triathlon through the '*valley of the shadow of death.*'

The guide probably saw that I was lost in my thoughts and asked, "How did your son die?"

"He died in a DUI accident in San Francisco." *Reality!*

"How old was he?"

"He was twenty-three."

"That is so young! I'm sorry for your loss."

I looked over at him. His work is dealing with survivors of the dead. *Reality...* Me.

"You said you haven't been here in a long time?"

"It has been about 17 years. The last time I was here was with his mother. We were visiting his grave together alone for the first time since he had died. There were so many young people, friends and relatives the day of the funeral."

I looked at the dates and realized that it had been twenty years since his untimely death. It seemed like almost another lifetime ago! I felt myself drifting off into memories when the groundskeeper spoke.

"Where do you live now?"

"I live in the foothills of the Sierra Mountains past Sacramento. I moved up from the Bay area about 5 years ago."

"Oh, I see. What do you do up there?"

"I work as a DUI counselor."

"So, you are helping other people avoid what happened to your son?"

"Yes, I'm trying."

"Well, it is good you are using your life experience to teach and help others. We see so many young people buried here because of driving under the influence."

Reality! He turned and walked back over the hill. I was alone in front of the head stone facing the grave *reality.*

I tried to imagine how he looked that day in the mortuary. I couldn't remember if it was an open casket. I was so numbed out. It was like a bad dream you cannot wake up from. Being an alcoholic/addict, I coped with more booze, pot and cocaine. No wonder I couldn't remember!

The end of the dash on the gravestone was engraved with the date: **1991**. It had been twenty years. I thought it had only been eighteen years. Now, the third *twenty-year act* of my life was ending; full circle... with me standing on my son's grave.

I do remember certain statements made that dark day: 'That's not the way it's supposed to be; Parents burying their children is not natural!'

Other parents would say, "I'm so sorry for your loss. I can't imagine what you are going through."

The main thing I always remembered was what my Mother said as the coffin was slowly lowered into the ground. "Mark, don't ever make me go through this with you!" I really didn't know what she meant at the time, but what she said eventually saved my life.

I looked across the lonely sloping hill full of gravesites. I thought of the dozens of his young, twenty-something friends at the funeral two decades ago. With the sleeping dead below my feet, I walked slowly back to the car where my friend Wendy was waiting. We had supported each other throughout the many years of dealing with life on life's terms. Sometimes life feels like a 'slippery slope'. You can slide right back into the drinking/using again... if you don't have a good support system.

I felt incredibly sad. Thank God that Wendy was with me. I approached the car and she gave me that look of concern.

"Are you OK?"

I lowered myself into the car. She put her hand on my shoulder.

"That was definitely a trip into the time capsule!"

I started the car and drove out of the cemetery and headed back on the freeway towards San Francisco. The pre-sunset flamingo pink clouds pointed westerly toward the Pacific Ocean.

My head was in the clouds of grey that were lower on the horizon. The grieving process is a continuing continuum. I gave a heavy sigh. "What a day Ms. Wendy."

The words to a Grateful Dead song played in the soundtrack of my mind: *What a Long Strange Trip It's Been!* The story that began in the 1960's, continued still; being written with a heavy hand, and a heavy heart.

Another song played through my mind: *Turn, Turn, Turn.* This song was written by Pete Seeger, and performed by the band named the "BYRDS" in the 1960's. The words were adapted from the bible in the book of Ecclesiastes. It was a big hit on the radio. It was permanently downloaded in my brain. Sometimes it would just start playing; TURN, TURN, TURN.

ECCLESIASTES 3

To everything (Turn, Turn, Turn)
there is a season, (Turn, Turn, Turn)
And a time to every purpose under heaven:
    A time to be born, A time to die
    A time to plant, A time to reap
    A time to kill, A time to heal
    A time to laugh, A time to weep
    A time to build up, A time to break down
    A time to dance, A time to mourn
    A time to cast away stones,
    A time to gather stones together
    A time of love, A time of hate
    A time of war, A time of peace

A time you may embrace, A time to refrain from embracing
A time to gain, A time to lose
A time to rend, A time to sew
A time for love, a time to hate
A time for peace, I swear it's not too late

"Mark, are you OK?"

"Yes, I was just spacing out a little bit."

"So, what do you have planned for the evening?"

"I'm going to go the hospital in San Francisco where my son died. I need to process what happened 20 years ago with my sober brain."

"I understand. You can take me home if you want."

We headed to her house. We talked about current family situations and how fast time has gone by. I walked her to her house and gave her a hug.

"Thanks for going with me to the cemetery."

"Sure Mark. Thanks for going with me to the memorial."

"OK Wendy, I'll call you next time I come down this way."

"Don't make it so long next time."

I went back to my car and drove off. I passed by the agency where I first worked as a counselor 14 years ago. I did my college internship there, and eventually was hired.

Back on the freeway towards San Francisco, the last light of sunset outlined the clouds over the Pacific. I could see the lights of the city and across the bay.

I drove down by the San Francisco Zoo and parked at the beach. One of the things I miss about living in the Bay Area is being able to watch the sun set down into the ocean. The sun fell and flattened out on the horizon. It looked like a golden disk sinking into the deep-blue abyss.

As the darkness blotted out the light of day, I headed toward San Francisco General Hospital... where my son died. If I was going to include this story in my book, I needed to refresh my memory. I would revisit the places where the events occurred.

CHAPTER 11
DARK NIGHT OF THE SOUL

Driving to San Bruno, the 'Airport City', where I went to High School. I stopped at the donut shop and got some coffee and donuts. Memories of the teenage years flooded my mind as I headed back to the freeway on-ramp for San Francisco. This was the same route I took on that fatal night; a good place to begin this part of the story. I parked in the hospital parking lot… and began to write.

A Night in Hell!

I got the call no one ever wants to get. It was my son's friend calling from a phone booth in San Francisco. In a frantic tone, he spoke. "Mark, David was just in an accident with his motorcycle! He is still alive and they are loading him into an ambulance!"

I immediately went into shock mode. "Where are they taking him?"

I could hear the ambulance siren fade off into the distance. Another siren was getting louder.

His friend yelled out, "Where are they taking him?"

A faint voice in the background replied, "San Francisco General Hospital."

"The other ambulance is here for his passenger. She is seriously injured too! They are going to San Francisco General. I'm going to follow the ambulance. I'll see you there."

I could hear chaotic voices and crying as he clanged the phone on the hook.

My party friends were watching me from the kitchen table.

Big Mickey looked concerned. "What happened Mark?"

"Oh my God, my son was just in an accident! They are taking him and his girlfriend to San Francisco General. Who can drive me there?"

We were all wasted. We had been partying all evening and now it was around midnight. Luckily Guitar George was there and he did not drink. "I can drive you Mark, let's go."

We ran out to the car and headed north on the Bayshore Freeway toward San Francisco. We passed the airport. It was about a 20-minute drive from the peninsula where I lived. I felt as though I was in slow-motion-time-warp. The shock and fear of the unknown smothered my mind in darkness.

When I saw Candlestick Park, I knew we were almost there. We pulled off the freeway at Army Street and turned right toward Mission Street. We approached the hospital; a big red brick building spread out along the whole block. There was a sign reading: **Comprehensive Emergency Medical Service Physician On Duty.** And: **Public Entrance,** with an arrow pointing to the parking lot, and a cross symbol followed by **EMERGENCY,** and another arrow pointing down the street. I was thankful George was driving through this confusing maze. Finally, a big red sign reading: **AMBULANCE ONLY.**

We pulled into the parking lot near the **EMERGENCY ENTRANCE** and parked. My friend looked at me with disbelief. "Are you ready for this?"

Nobody is really ready for the events that unfolded next on this dark San Francisco night.

We got out of the car and walked toward the **Emergency Entrance** door, just as an ambulance pulled up to the **ER** dock. My son's friends parked their motorcycles and ran towards the ambulance. The security guard directed us to the **ER** entrance.

My son's friend who called me looked at me with shock in his eyes. "He's gonna' be alright. David's strong, he'll survive this!"

We all walked down a long well-lit hall and made a right to where the ambulance was. The medics pulled him out and placed him on the gurney, and hurriedly rolled him down the hall of light. I thought I saw his spirit hovering over his body like a floating balloon as they disappeared around the corner.

We were asked to go into the waiting room. I was surrounded by a group of his friends. They were all so young; in their early twenties. They were talking about the events of that evening. They had all been drinking at a restaurant bar in San Francisco. My son had consumed quite a few drinks, more than he was used to drinking. His drug of choice was marijuana, but because he was going to be drug tested to enter a rehab in a couple of weeks, he was drinking instead.

He and his friends had left the restaurant and got on their motorcycles. David and a lady friend were on his bike together. His friend described what happened next.

"They were going down Divisadero Street really fast. It was a rainy, slippery night. A car ran a red light entering into the intersection... and David's motorcycle T-boned the car. He flew over the car with no helmet on, and came to a stop head first right into a steel light post. His lady friend passenger was stopped by the car. It was horrible!"

The waiting room was full of his sobbing lady friends. The young men were reassuring each other that he was going to be alright.

I stepped outside to get some fresh air and process what was happening. I caught my breath standing in the cool, frigid air.

I was picturing the accident scenario on the blank screen of my mind. It was not a pretty picture to envision.

A security guard approached me and asked if I was OK. I asked him where the nearest bar was. He said down on Portrero Street. I looked at the time. It was almost two o'clock. I started running down the street as fast as I could. All I could think about was how much I needed a drink.

I saw the *Jack's Cocktails* sign on the corner with a martini symbol below the name Jack's. A double Jack Daniels is what I would order, or maybe two… before final call at two. That would help me make it through the night.

Just as I crossed the street, I saw the bar door close. I sprinted to the door and heard the lock click. I panicked! I frantically knocked on the door.

A loud voice inside responded, "We are closed."

I pleaded. "Please open, I just need one drink!"

"Come back at six in the morning."

"You don't understand, my son is in the ER and I really need a drink, please!"

"No, we're closed. Come back in the morning."

I knocked again in desperation. The lights in the bar turned off. Everything was dark.

I never wanted a drink so badly in all my life. I couldn't believe I missed it by a minute.

I stood on the corner in shock and disbelief. The reality of the hospital was down the street… waiting for me. I slowly walked through the dark misty night. I felt numb; but not numb enough. I didn't want to feel at all.

As I entered the ER parking lot, my son's mother was getting out of her husband's car. She walked into the hospital. I stood outside the ER door. His mother was surrounded by her son's friends. I felt like this was the end. I didn't want to feel at all. It was going to be all pain all night.

I opened the door and entered the waiting room… permeated with emotional and psychological pain. Life would never be the same. There was an atmosphere of trauma thick as blood. The brightly lit waiting room was glaring with the reality of the unknown; waiting and wondering what the damage was. Crying and sighing; waiting and not knowing.

His friends were consoling his mother. "He'll be alright. He's strong. He'll make it through this."

Wishful words in the waiting room. Waiting through those moments of silence, and wading through those moments of anguish, I couldn't begin to imagine the pain she was suffering. I was a distant dad through the first half of his life. She gave birth to him, there from the beginning with her only child, her beloved son. The labor, the birth pains, and now overwhelmed with sorrow! He was her baby, her toddler, her young boy, taking him to kindergarten, seeing him through elementary school. She saw his pre-teen middle school days leading him to a young man in high school. She witnessed his blossoming and blooming to his eventual graduation pictures as a handsome young man. Sadly, I was not there for the first 12 years of his life.

The sound of another siren startled me out of my stupor. The stark reality of this dark night of pain, while waiting and waiting, in this waiting room… was upon us.

And so, the traumatic night of hell continued on. I could feel myself sobering up. I took a deep breath and lit a cigarette: the only drug I had then, nicotine. I was a nervous addict feeling withdrawals. Nicotine withdrawals happen fast. In a couple of hours your body starts craving the drug. In times of stress you smoke even more. I smoked a couple more cigarettes and wondered what awaited.

His mother walked out of the waiting room. I couldn't believe the look of sadness on her face. It killed me inside to see her.

As I hugged her she said, "The doctors want to talk to us."

"O.K."

I put my cigarette out in the full ashtray and reluctantly entered through the doors again, this time with his mother.

Her husband was there. My girlfriend was also there. We all walked down the long hall together, following a nurse.

We silently rode the elevator to the second floor and waited in another room near the Administration Offices. In an awful silence… we awkwardly sat.

I heard a song in my head play over and over in the terrible silence. "Turn, Turn, Turn." It was the BYRDS 1960's rock band version; the ringing electric twelve string with the lyrics from the Bible book of Ecclesiastes. *"To everything, turn, turn, turn; there is a season turn, turn, turn;* and a *time to every purpose, under heaven."* Ecclesiastes scripture singing, ringing in my head.

Nightmare News

We returned to the room where our other loved ones were waiting. They looked at us with wondering eyes.

"What did they say?"

I answered the young woman who asked. "They said that the best doctors have him in surgery and they will let us know what is going on."

I heard them consoling each other; "He'll be alright. He's strong. He'll make it. There's still hope."

I looked across the room. My son's mother was sitting next to her husband. He looked at me for the first time without hate in his eyes. He helped his wife stand up and they left the room. I never imagined we would all be sitting in the same room together. My girlfriend held my hand and we followed them down the long, well-lit hall of darkness.

Pastoral pictures hung on the walls of these halls. We passed many doors to many rooms. One room had a sign on over the door that read: Welcome to the Multi-lingual Chapel. Chaplain available between the hours of 9 am to 5 pm Monday through Friday.

I didn't know what day or time it was. The door was locked. We walked on into the "night in hell!"

We returned to the ER waiting room.

Our son's friends surrounded us full of tears and fears.

The sound track played on:

Turn, Turn, Turn
"A time to embrace, and a time to be far from embraces."
Ecclesiastes 3:5

I stepped out into the dark depressed night. The sliver of the moon peaked through the black clouds. I felt like a was in a Van Gogh picture: Starry, Starry Nights. The song of that name written by Don Mclean popped into my mind. Then, the famous song he wrote, "The Day the Music Died" followed in the ongoing musical of tragedy. I lit a cigarette and blew the bluish smoke into the night air.

The background music of our lives plays on, like the soundtrack of a movie as the scenes change and the stage is rearranged. X marks the spot where you stand in this human drama play. And the band plays on. *"To everything there is a season; A time to laugh a time to cry."*

I cried for the first time that awful night. In my solitude behind the hospital, I was hiding my feelings of weakness and powerlessness. I felt broken, but I could not break down that night. I had to stay strong. I lit another cigarette.

The whiskey and beer I had drunk earlier that night were metabolizing out of my body through my heavy sighs. I did not feel alright. My body and brain were swirling down the drain of dark despair.

Would I ever be able to repair the damage done in this life, and the consequences of my choices and actions? At the age of 41, had it all come undone? I had nowhere to run. I was always able to fight or take flight into the night. Now I was paralyzed in place; frozen and unable to cope... with no hope. Hopeless, and powerless, and stunned to the bone. I felt like a drone; empty of spirit and full of pain.

Again, the verses:

Turn, Turn, Turn
"A time to rend, a time to sew."
Ecclesiastes 3:7

Now you know, now you know.

The night of hell continued in a foggy haze. I flashed back to the last time I talked to my son. He took me for a ride on his new fast motorcycle. He had a helmet on the back of his bike, but did not wear it. I sat behind him on the bike and away we went. I realized why they called them "rice rockets!" It was a lot quicker than the Hondas we had back in the 60's.

We cut in and out of traffic, barely making a few spaces between cars. The rear-view mirror hit another rear-view mirror on a car in passing.

I flashed back again to riding with my friend on his brand new 650 Honda when we were in High School. I had a Vespa motor scooter that didn't go fast enough to go on the freeway. Now we were on a real motorcycle. He drove like a maniac and I felt powerless because my life was in his hands. We were young and wild on a motorcycle. What a thrill!

After riding four blocks with my son, he pulled over to adjust his rear-view mirror. "Do you want to drive Dad?"

"No thanks son, I haven't ridden since high school."

I stopped riding after my third crash on a Triumph motorcycle. I scraped my left leg, turning a corner and slipping on an oil spill. That was it for me. I only rode dirt bikes after that.

As I took what would be my final ride with my son, I held onto his hips and noticed how strong and sturdy his young body was. He was buffed after being in jail for the last several months. He was also bigger than I… not hard to do, as I'm five foot five. He was a prime 23-year-old man now.

We pulled up in front of my house. I was glad that "thrill ride was over!" As I got off the bike I looked at him. "Boy, that's a fast bike you got there." He chuckled at me, knowing I was a little shaken' up. We talked about what he was going to do now that he was out of jail. He did time for out-running cops with his motorcycle for years. When they finally caught him, they decided to teach him a lesson. I visited him several times when he was incarcerated.

"I'm going to rehab as part of the early release deal the D.A. gave me. That's why I'm not smokin' weed. I'm waiting for a bed to be available at Project 90 in a week or two. To get in, I need to test clean for drugs. I have a chance to turn my life around. I'm going to start a new, legal business. My friends and I are going to get a fleet of limousines and go legit."

"I'm so happy to hear that. Project 90 and their ninety-day program have a good reputation for turning men around after getting out of jail. You have a chance to change your life around son!"

"Oh, and Dad, speaking of life, I just wanted to thank you and Mom for not aborting me and giving me life."

I gave him a hug.

"Well, I'm off to the city with my friends. It was good to see ya'!"

He mounted the motorcycle.

"Be sure to wear your helmet."

"Yeh, I will. The motorcycle helmet law starts in 5 weeks. It's not illegal to not wear one yet."

He revved up the engine and took off, doin' a wheelie half way down the street with no helmet on. It was still attached to the back seat. That was the last time I saw him until tonight. I was worried about him then. That's what parents do. Now… I was more than worried about him.

He wasn't really a drinker. His friends said he slammed down quite a few drinks that night before the accident. His drug of choice was marijuana, but since he was getting drug tested he was drinking instead. I thought about how unfair the laws were. If pot wasn't illegal, maybe he wouldn't have been drinking and driving. I don't know. Pot stays in your system for up to a month in a drug test. My thoughts started to scramble.

I could feel the morning coming. The black, rainy, drizzly shrouds of clouds, were turning slowly grey. I wondered what would happen on this cold San Francisco day. I could hear the freeway traffic. Mission Street came alive with church bells ringing through the air. Was it Sunday? I really didn't care. It was a day I did not want to face, but it was harshly staring me in the face; another day in the human race.

In and out and all about; the morning shift hospital workers arriving, the night shift leaving. My friend came out to get me.

"The Doctors want to have a consultation with the parents. You need to come in now."

I nervously lit another cigarette, and in a huff, took a puff. Puff the Magic Dragon flashed into my mind. Another song from childhood that always made me sad.

"O.K., one more puff and I guess I'm ready."

We entered the ER again. I followed my friend to the elevator and up to the second floor. We went into the room we had been in hours before. I sat down across from his Mother. The Doctor came in.

"The surgery is finished. He is in a comatose state. You can see him now. He is hooked up to life support. Follow me, and I will talk to you after."

To Everything Turn, Turn, Turn

There he was; lying in a bed with a white cloth wrapped around the top of his head. White sheets covered his body. Not a sight of blood of which covered him when he arrived on the gurney last night.

Tubes were in his mouth and nose. Needles were in his arms. Machines with dials and meters, were measuring vital signs of life. It was amazing and stunning to see all this technology that could keep people alive.

His Mother leaned over next to him and kissed him on the forehead.

She touched his face, and then ran her fingers over his lips.

I felt frozen... and stood there like a statue.

She slowly walked around the bed examining him from head to toe. His feet were sticking out from the sheets. She touched them, and then... looked at me.

"Come over here and see his feet."

I slowly stepped to the end of the bed. As I looked at his feet, I felt light in the head. The bright lights started to fade to grey. My strong sturdy body gave way. I felt faint and started to fall amidst it all. I fell to the floor at the foot of his bed. I was looking up at his Mother as the nurses asked for help. They surrounded me and lifted me onto the gurney right next to him. I felt helpless as I laid there next to my son's bed. How could this happen. I needed to be strong and support his Mother through this.

To everything Turn, Turn, Turn

I felt like an autumn leaf; detached from the tree. I laid there helplessly. How could this happen to me? I was always the strong oldest son of the family?

The nurses took my pulse and blood pressure. They checked my eyes and asked: "When was the last time you ate?"

The nurse turned to speak to my son's Mother. "It's probably low blood pressure from not eating."

They brought me some orange juice in a small paper cup. She placed it to my lips. "Drink some of this please."

Eventually the light got brighter and I could see clearly again. This was not a bad dream; this was reality. I was lying in a gurney next to my son in an intensive care unit. I was going through alcohol withdrawal and the nurses didn't know it; but I sure was feeling it.

I looked at the clock in the nurses' station. It was 6 o'clock in the morning. As soon as I could get off this gurney and walk, I could go straight down to Jack's and down a couple of shots of Jack. That's what I knew I really needed. I did not need a nurse; I needed to nurse a beer after a couple shots of whiskey. I laid there waiting my Turn, Turn, Turn.

As soon as I could I slid off the side of the gurney. The nurses ran over to me.

"Are you feeling O.K. now?"

They helped me over to a chair and started checking my vitals. "Just sit here for a minute, O.K.?"

They checked my pulse and blood pressure. "He's stabilized now."

My son's Mother looked at me, and then back at her son.

Another nurse approached us. "The doctors would like to talk to both of you when you are ready."

I sat there for a minute and then slowly stood up. I looked at our son and then his Mother with her hand on his forehead.

A social worker came into the room with her clip board. "The doctors will meet with you in the consultation room down the hall in about twenty minutes."

Not enough time to go down to the bar, I thought. I felt soberer by the minute. My head was pounding. As soon as this was over I will get a bloody Mary. That's what I would need for this "hell-atious" hangover.

The nurses helped me to the door, one on each side. We passed my son lying there, all hooked up to those machines. I felt myself leaning and the nurse supported me.

I kept thinking, 'I'm supposed to be strong. I'm not supposed to be weak!' I needed help from the floor to the door, and I wasn't even drunk!

To Everything Turn, Turn, Turn:
"There is an appointed time for everything,
and a time for every affair under the heavens."
Ecclesiastes 3:1

The Morning of Reckoning

They took us down another long hallway. The bright lights hurt my eyes. I don't remember if my girlfriend was with me, or if my son's Mother's husband was there. I just remember his Mother next to me. It was like we were sleep-walking down a long endless hall with many rooms.

We entered another room and sat down across from each other; flooded with over-whelming emotions. We looked at each other. She appeared to not be doing so well either. Her head was hanging down and her drooping eyes were filled with incredible sadness. Denial was trying to tell me this was not really happening.

Reality opened the door. The doctor came in.

"I'm sorry to inform you that the brain surgeons have determined that your son is brain-dead. We have him on life support for now. We had our best surgeons operating and we did the best we could do. A Psychiatrist will be in soon to talk to you about your options."

He left. We were alone again. She looked pale. She was very silent and I didn't know what to say. I walked over to her and placed my hand on her shoulder. She cried. I died inside.

Unbearable sadness. No words to describe the feeling. To Everything Turn, Turn, Turn... played through my mind in the silence.

"A time to rend, and a time to sew;
a time to be silent and a time to speak."
Ecclesiastes 3:7

The Psychiatrist entered the room and told us how sorry she was about what had happened. She looked at me and asked me to follow her into an adjoining room as a Social Worker came in to console his Mother.

The Psychiatrist asked me to sit down. I sat. She pulled up a chair in front of me and looked intently into my eyes.

"Do you know where you are?"

"Yes, San Francisco General Hospital."

"What day is it?"

"I think its Thursday morning."

"Did the Doctor inform you of your son's condition?"

"Yes."

"What else did he say?"

"He told us our son was brain-dead!"

She looked me straight in my bloodshot eyes, and very seriously said: "A decision needs to be made concerning your son. His Mother does not appear to be able to make this decision, and so... we are asking you. Your son is on life support and brain dead. The Doctors want to know if they should unhook him from life support. There is a risk that he may die soon after he is removed from this life support. Because he is brain dead, he will stop breathing without the machine. I will give you some time to think about it. I will come back to talk to you in a little while."

The psychiatrist placed her hand on my shoulder. She suggested I consider what I would want for myself if I was in that state of being. She left me alone in the room.

To Everything Turn, Turn, Turn:

"A time to give birth, and a time to die;
A time to plant, and a time to uproot the plant."
Ecclesiastes 3:2

How do you possibly make a life and death decision? I tried to imagine if that was me in that hospital bed all hooked up to machines. What would I want for myself?

I thought of my friend who, a few years earlier, had been paralyzed in an accident on the Golden Gate Bridge. He was hit by a drunk driver. He was a very talented guitar player, very lively and always on the move. He came to visit me after the accident… in a wheelchair. I didn't know it at the time, but, he was doing the rounds to see his friends before dying. I could understand his reason to not want to live. He could make the decision for himself, but my son could not. What would he want? What would I want?

I knew if it was me, I would not want to be hooked to machines keeping me alive. I would want to be able to die naturally without this medical technology.

My brain was in pain with these thoughts. How can anyone make a decision like this? No one should have to be in a position to make this kind of choice.

The psychiatrist returned. "The doctors have assured me that your son is definitely brain dead. If they leave him on life support, he will exist in a vegetative state. I know this probably is the hardest decision you may ever make. If you need some more time, I understand.

"No, I would not want this for myself, and I don't think my son would either."

She held my hand. "O.K., I will let the doctors know."

So, the word went out that they would unplug him in 3 days. After he was to be removed from the life support, it was unknown how long it would be until his eventual demise. The only thing that is certain, said the doctors; He would not awake and it would be like dying in your sleep.

I flashed back to twenty years ago, when the first family member I knew had died; my Grandfather. At the funeral, the relatives were saying how lucky he was to have died in his sleep. "The best way to die," they said. I was at the funeral with my father as he watched when they laid his father to rest. My aunts gathered around the coffin crying. It was so very sad.

I remember watching President Kennedy's funeral on the television. That was also sad, but he was not family. Grandpa's death hit home.

A social worker came into visit me. "Are you O.K.?"

I wasn't, but I said yes.

She tried to console me. "You have made the right decision for your son. With such massive head trauma, he is medically dead, as there is no activity in his central-nervous-system. You are allowing him to move on and leave his broken body behind. He felt no pain in the accident, and the last thing he knew was that he was riding his motorcycle through the streets of San Francisco with his pretty girlfriend on the back."

"How is his girlfriend doing?"

"She has serious injuries, but is expected to recover. The sanctuary is open now. His Mother is there with friends and other family. You can join them. The chaplain is also there."

> *"A time to seek and a time to lose;*
> *A time to keep, and a time to cast away."*
> Ecclesiastes 3:6

Fade to grey for the rest of the day. I don't remember much from that point on. I was in a crazed daze. I know I finally got my drink. I was now on the brink. I don't remember when I reached the black-out stage. It all became a blur; as though I had been sucked into a big black hole!

I am sure my "party friends" managed to allow me to self-medicate myself to sleep.

When I finally did become conscious, I didn't want to be.

The answering machine was blinking. I pushed the play button and opened the fridge. I needed some hangover medicine. I opened a beer and sat down at the table. There were empty bottles of booze and smeared mirrors. The stench of cigarettes and beer permeated the kitchen air. I didn't care.

The messages began to play. My family: my sisters, brother and Mother. My friends and his friends. Questions and condolences. More messages than I could possibly respond to.

I didn't know if it was Thanksgiving, or the day after. I wanted reality to stay outside the door. I did know that I could not cope without more alcohol. I lit up part of a joint from the ashtray and took a big hit. I held the smoke in as long as I could, and then broke down in a coughing fit.

One of the messages I feared, I heard.

"David was just unhooked from life support. We are all here at the hospital. Are you going to join us?"

Reality opened the door. This was not a dream I could awaken from. I was awake and conscious. The messages played on.

"Mark, where are you?"

I sat there looking at the party table. The party was over.

The next message was it.

"Mark, David died. Where are you?"

Where was I? I was lost… I was gone. I was dying inside to the deepest, darkest, blues song dirge. I chain smoked and drank on and on and on. I tried to numb myself to the world outside the door. I just lay on the living room floor staring at the ceiling. His life in pictures was flashing through my brain; two months old, then two years old, twelve, twenty-two and so much more. Suddenly, reality was knocking on my door.

I rose slowly off the floor and stumbled to the door. I was glad to see it was my friend Mikey.

"Mark, your sister has been calling me. Everyone is worried about you. I told her I would come over and check on you. Are you O.K.?"

"No!" I cried. I lay back down on the floor.

"A time to weep, a time to laugh;
A time to mourn, and a time to dance.
Ecclesiastes 3:4

I definitely wasn't dancing or laughing. Depression crushed me like a giant granite boulder.

I missed a lot in my life. I had heard people say to me that I would miss my own funeral. I missed my graduation because I wouldn't cut my hair. The principal would not let me get my diploma or graduate on stage unless I cut it. It was his last attempt to make me comply with his demands. I would not do it, even if my Mother wanted me to do.

I told the principal, "Mail it to me!

The night of my missed graduation, I was drinking with some friends. I didn't care. I also missed the Junior Prom and Senior Prom for the same reason. I didn't care, I partied on.

I reasoned: It's the principle of it. He will not win!

I missed school when I was suspended. I didn't care. I didn't want to be in school anyway. As long as I could attend the minimum to graduate for my Mother. That was all I needed.

I missed the first half of his life. I missed his childhood. I was there in the last half of his life. Now I was missing his death!

I was missing on Thanksgiving. I was missing in action. M.I.A. The only thing I wanted to miss was my misery. No matter how much I self-medicated, I couldn't escape myself. No one could save me from myself. I was my own worst enemy.

Turn, Turn, Turn
A time to kill, and a time to heal;
A time to break down, and a time to build.
Ecclesiastes 3:3

BROKEN DOWN

I had won a lot of battles in my life: The battle with the school; the battle with the school board who had to overturn my suspension for long hair; the battle with the draft board over the war; the battle with the court system for having two joints when it was a felony. There were consequences for some of these battles that I paid for playing. I was willing to pay to play. I chose my battles well. "To hell with them!" was my rebellious attitude.

But now I was broken. Losing left and right, with nothing left to fight. Broken on the floor, I couldn't fight no more. My body, soul and spirit were bruised and broken.

My friend Mikey sat down at the table. There was someone there when I didn't care, mostly about myself. I lay there; 'tore up from the ground up.'

"I brought you some bread my Mother made. Come on, get up and sit. Eat some bread. It's good."

Instead of offering me vodka and coke, he offered me bread and hope. "When your sister gets back from her honeymoon, she said she will come right over. She wants you to call your Mom. Come on Mark, get up and eat some bread."

Mikey was big. I knew I could lean on him if I felt faint. He walked over and reached out his hand.

I sat up on the floor. My head throbbed at the temples. I felt too week to stand, so I took hold of his big strong hand. The telephone rang and I got to my feet. I felt like I had just gone 9 rounds with Muhammad Ali.

The phone rang all day. Ring, ring, ring. I was like a boxer in the ring and when the referee rang the bell, I fell. I couldn't go on. I just wanted to hide in my room, sleep in my tomb, go back to the womb.

Mikey handed me the phone. He was wearing the Santa hat he always wore the month between Thanksgiving and Christmas.

"Mark, your sister's on the phone."

I lit up a cigarette and took a drag. I reluctantly put the phone up to my ear. The process was starting… reality calling.

"Oh good Mikey's there. I'll be coming over there as soon as I can. Eat something and get ready. Did you call Mom?"

"No not yet."

"O.K. I'll call her and let her know you're alright. I'll call you right back. Let me talk to Mikey."

I handed the phone back to Mikey.

"Not too good", he said as he looked at me worriedly.

I hadn't looked in the mirror yet. What did he see as he looked at me? I must have looked a mess.

I got up, holding on to the table; the only way I was really able. I walked to the bathroom and closed the door. I saw the man in the mirror, looking back at me, like he had always done for the last 40 years of personal awareness. The man in the mirror looked worried too. So, sullen and sad, he knew what he had to do. Run the water, wash that face, but……you cannot wash your hands of the human race. Don't throw in the towel. Clean yourself up and get ready for another round.

Turn, Turn, Turn
A time to cast away stones,
A time to gather stones together.
Ecclesiastes 3:5

Face to face with myself! A self-reality check. Not a pretty picture framed by the medicine cabinet mirror: The damage done at age

41. I didn't want to look too close, so I ran the water and washed my face. I looked at the shower and stayed away. I knew I would fall in the stall. I grabbed a towel and dried my face. I knew I would have to pace myself: One step at a time. Lord have mercy on me.

I slowly returned to the kitchen. Mikey sat there like Santa come early. I was never ready for Christmas. Shopping at the last minute, dropping my presents at my sister's to wrap as I arrived late, as usual, to family gatherings. I did not even want to think about the holidays.

Mikey looked at me and took on the manager role, since he could tell I had become unmanageable. "There is a message on the answering machine from the singer in the band. You have a Christmas Party to play tomorrow night. He said to wear the red tie and cummerbund."

I looked at the long dark closet next to my room. I knew my tuxedo was in there, I had worn it at the country club last weekend. The red tie and cummerbund were there from last year. I wanted to go in the closet and hide. I did not want to face the day. I did not want to talk to anyone. I did not want to face reality. I just wanted to escape from myself.

I had lost and at what a cost. I knew I would continue to pay. The party was over and it was time to pay the piper. Bankrupt in spirit and soul, I did not have enough to pay the trolls toll. Oh no, oh no, oh no!!!

Turn, Turn, Turn

CHAPTER 12

GOOD NEWS

I am a recovering drunk driver! I reached what they call in the 12 step programs... 'my bottom'. It took about 4 years after my son's **death by DUI,** to finally turn my life around. I had first gone to Alcoholics Anonymous with my friend who was going to stop drinking. At that time, I was definitely in the pre-contemplation stage of no change. I didn't think I had a problem like the people in the meeting. I never had a DUI. I got arrested for two joints when I was younger, but nothing major. I never lost a job because of drinking, or any of the things those people were talking about. I didn't need help.

A couple of years later, a girlfriend told me if I didn't go to AA and stop drinking, she would leave me. I went for a couple of weeks. I would sneak into the meetings late and hide behind a plant in the corner and leave early. These people were really sick, and I was not like them. I told my girlfriend that I wasn't really an alcoholic and that I would just cut down and control my drinking. I told her I would drink in moderation and not get drunk. Two drinks a day maximum.

Eventually she left me because my plan did not work too well. I would drink two drinks, but they were Long Island Ice Teas, or

151 Rum and cokes. Then she left and I could drink as much as I wanted again. I decided she was my problem.

The next girlfriend told me if I would just snort cocaine and not drink I would be better. I tried this… but I didn't' like the jittery feeling of just the coke without the alcohol. I went back to AA and tried just smoking pot without the coke and alcohol. That only lasted three days.

I decided I needed to have a girlfriend that liked to party as much as I did; or one that wouldn't complain about my drinking. I found some 'party girls' along the way, but these relationships were not serious, and quite depressing. When the alcohol and drugs ran out, and the party was over, I was alone and depressed again. I was treading through shallow waters towards the deep end.

My career seemed to be going good. I had a record contract and was partying like a rock star, with the rock stars. Late night parties and sometimes all-nighters were taking their toll on me. I was afraid to look into the mirror.

I was not functioning too well. My next girlfriend suggested I go back to AA again and give it a try. I managed to cut down enough to prove to her I would be OK. I would drink two beers a day, but they were 16-ounce Malt Liquors. This only lasted a couple of weeks. I would go to the store to get some milk and bread, and buy a 24-ounce Malt Liquor. I'd drink it in my car in the church parking lot, then I would go back in the house. When I played gigs, I started drinking and partying more and more.

I was starting to neglect my health and well-being. I wasn't taking care of business, and I was having problems 'keeping it together.' I tried AA again, and had a couple of weeks of sobriety. I started wondering if I could stop to even save my life. My life was falling apart! I became full of anxiety and fear of losing everything. I wasn't even sure if I cared enough to stop.

One day I came home and found a note on the kitchen table from one of my best friends. She wrote that she was worried about me, and perhaps I needed some professional help. I just stared at the letter... and wondered if she was right. I had heard stories in AA that reminded me of some of the things I was going through. I couldn't believe that I might possibly be like them. I was starting to contemplate that possibility. I was moving from pre-contemplation, to the contemplation stage. I was considering going back to AA, not because a girlfriend thought I should go, but because I was realizing I might need help!

It was the holidays again. I had a bunch of gigs to play. I just played and partied on, with the thought that maybe the party was really over. I had tried to quit several times, but I kept going. When I played the last Christmas party of the season at the country club, one of the band members gave me a Christmas present. I went home and opened it up. It was a big bottle of Irish liquor. I just looked at it on the table where I had partied for years. I was so tired I went to my room and passed out with my tuxedo on. I awoke in the middle of the night and took off my tuxedo. I went to the bathroom and took some aspirin.

I woke up Christmas morning to the sound of my sister's voice on the answering machine, asking me if I was coming to Christmas dinner with the family.

I got out of bed and made some coffee. I opened the fridge and took out a cold beer to drink while waiting for the coffee. I knew it would help my hangover. I felt like I had been dragged down the road behind a pickup truck! I guzzled the beer and went into the bathroom. There was that mirror reflecting my being back at me with serious reality. The mirror wasn't broken, but, I was. I washed my face and took inventory to see if I was presentable enough to fake being OK in front of my mother. My brother and sister would be there, and they were both clean and sober and in the program.

I drank some coffee and remembered I had told one of my musician friends, who had no family, that he could come with me to my family Christmas. He had lots of pot, so I could make it with him through the day OK. Since my son died four years ago, I would always make the trip with him.

I called him and told him I would pick him up in a half hour. I took a shower and got dressed. I was starting to almost feel normal again. I looked in the mirror and appeared to be good enough to make the trip.

I picked up my friend. He got in the car and put his seat belt on.

"Merry Christmas," he said joyfully. He showed me the cigarette pack full of marijuana joints. "This should be enough for the road!"

"Well Merry Christmas to you," I said happily after seeing the pot. He always had the 'good stuff.' I'll get some gas, then we can fire one up."

I found an open gas station and began to pump the gas. I noticed that my bald tires had steel sticking out of the sides. I wondered if I could drive 400 miles on those tires. I hadn't paid attention to the wear and tear on my tires, or on myself! We got on the freeway and headed toward the Bay Bridge. As we crossed the bridge, I hoped we would not get a flat in the middle. My friend fired up a joint and we kept going.

When we reached Berkeley, I heard the sound of the steel belted tires, actually hitting the wheel cover of the car, and decided I better take the University Exit and check it out. The steel belts were definitely a bad sign that the tires would not make it the whole trip. I got back in the car and my friend looked at me with his quizzical look.

I knew he would be disappointed with what I was going to say. "We aren't going to be able to make the trip this year. The tire treads are sticking out. Hopefully we can make it back across the bridge to San Francisco."

We headed back across the bridge. I prayed we would make it home OK. We smoked another joint when we made it back to San Francisco.

I dropped my friend off and apologized to him. I went home and called my sister. I told her my tires were bald and that I felt sick anyway.

"OK Mark, I'll let mom know you're not coming. Are you still going to AA?"

"No, not anymore."

"Well, maybe you should go back and try again. This time find a sponsor to help you work on the steps. It worked for me and your brother."

"OK, I'll think about it. Tell everyone Merry Christmas for me."

"Alright Mark, get some rest and I'll call you tomorrow."

I hung up the phone and opened another beer. I opened my Christmas present from the band and poured a drink. I would just drink myself asleep and escape from my misery. I was finally alone and didn't have to entertain anyone. I was relieved that I wasn't going to my families this Christmas. I didn't really want them to see me in this condition. I was a mess. Partying for four years like there's no tomorrow had really taken a toll on my well-being! I needed a long rest. I had enough beer and alcohol so that I didn't have to go anywhere. My next gig wasn't until New Year's Eve.

I cleaned the cocaine left on the table from the last party and mixed it with the roaches into a joint. I began to smoke myself into oblivion. I really didn't care anymore. I was alone and I was glad I was alone. I had played so many Holiday parties in the last month, trying to act like I was this merry musician helping everyone else be merry. The truth of it was: I was suffering from major depression and the parties and partying were not working anymore. I knew I needed help. I was helpless!

I drank some more, then ate some fruit cake so I wouldn't be drinking on an empty stomach. I went into the living room and sat on the couch under the picture of Jesus, with several people eating and drinking around a table with Him. This picture had been given to my sister by my mother, who had bought it from someone that said it was from a church. Supposedly, it had been instrumental in helping people heal. I hung it there when I moved in and never really paid much attention to it. I would walk past it, and not want to look at it; because I knew my life style was not one to make Jesus very happy with me.

I drank straight from the bottle of alcohol... until I passed out on the couch. I woke up several hours later to the sound of someone leaving message of Merry Christmas on the answering machine. It was still Christmas.

The sun was going down. The last rays of light shined through the window and illuminated the painting of Jesus. I noticed how the light shined through the window onto the painting, and Jesus image seemed to glow. I gazed at the picture as I lay there in a stupor on the couch. I reached for the bottle and took another drink. I pondered the picture until it was the dark of night.

I felt as though Jesus was watching me in my misery. I prayed to Jesus to help me. If anyone could help me, it must be Jesus. I knew he would forgive me, even though I couldn't forgive myself. I begged on my knees for His forgiveness in my drunken, broken, state of mind. I couldn't go on living a Godless life.

It took me three days to finish the alcohol. I told Jesus when it was all gone I would try to quit again, with Him as my higher power. On the third day, I went to Alcoholics Anonymous in the evening... and I never drank again.

It wasn't easy. Going through detox from alcohol was horrible. My party friends returned from their family Christmas events and New Year's was on its way. They wanted to party, and my house was the party house. My blind drummer roommate was home, and he was keeping the party going with all of our friends. I told them that I was going to AA again and that this time I was seriously trying to quit. They asked me if I was going to give up pot too. I told them no, but I was going to give up cocaine and speed. The party went on until New Year's Eve. I smoked pot, but no alcohol or cocaine.

I had a gig, as usual, playing a New Year's Eve party in San Francisco. As I put my tuxedo on, my friends were partying in the kitchen, as usual. Most of them lived with their parents still, so my place was the place to go party. I grabbed my guitar and took a hit from the joint they were smokin'… and headed off to the city.

As I drove down the coast, I thought about last year when I had this same gig. I had been going to AA for about a month, once a week, trying to stop my girlfriend from leaving me. She left me anyway, so I was single again. I had picked up the guitar player, and he asked me to stop at a liquor store so he could buy some beer for after the gig. He knew I was trying to stop drinking. He said he would take it home and drink it later. I agreed to let him keep it in my car while we played at the club.

We played the first two sets and I stayed sober, watching everyone around me drinking and celebrating. It was twenty to midnight when we took a break. The waiters were coming on stage with plates full of champagne glasses. I actually refused it. I was doing so good so far.

At the break, I walked outside to get away. My mind started thinking about the beer in the car. My mind was saying to me that it was New Year's Eve… and I deserved to have a drink. No one would know. I decided to go to the car and drink two beers before the countdown to midnight.

I got in the car and pulled two beers from the backseat. The first one tasted way different than the non-alcoholic beers I had been drinking for the last month. I realized the difference as I guzzled the beer and opened another. When I finished the second one, I decided I had time for a third one. Hey, it was New Year's: Celebrate. I put the first two empty beer cans between the door and the car seat. As I finished the third beer, I saw the guitar player come out of the club looking for me.

"Come on in. We're waiting for you to do the countdown!"

I opened the door and the beer cans noisily fell out onto the pavement. He looked at me with his weird grin.

"I thought you quit! Oh well, come on, we're going to be late for the countdown!"

I sang Celebration at midnight, and drank champagne for the rest of the night. After the gig, some pretty girls from L.A. wearing fishnet stockings asked us if we knew where to get some coke. Of course, we did! Later that night, the after-hours party began, on a houseboat in the San Francisco Bay. When the sun came up that New Year's Day, I watched from the deck and thought about how this was going to be the first New Year's Eve I was not going to drink and party.

Here I was again! When the cocaine ran out, the girls from L.A ran out, and here I was all burnt out. I had heard someone say at one of the AA meetings: 'when you get a head full of AA, the party is ruined.' The party was definitely over; and the New Year had just begun.

This time, I didn't have the guitar player and the beer with me. I might have a chance to really stay sober this time. I was very uncomfortable at the countdown to midnight, but I made it through to the New Year without drinking.

When I got home, my party friends were in the kitchen celebrating. I smoked some pot with them, and went to bed before the sun came up.

I had only been sober for one week and I decided to keep going to AA. I was on the 'marijuana maintenance' program. I would smoke a couple of joints with my friends, and then go to the AA meetings. I learned that there were a couple of others on the 'marijuana maintenance' program.

When I had been off the alcohol a couple of weeks, I had to get the tail light fixed on my car. I went to visit a mechanic friend to change the bulb for me. He asked me if I wanted a beer. I told him no and that I was going to go to an AA meeting in a little while.

He asked me if I wanted to do a line of coke. I said no again, and he said, "AA's just for alcohol, right. So why don't you do a line of coke then."

It made sense to me... so I snorted a line as he fixed my car. I drove off down the road to go home, and wait for the AA meeting that would start in a couple of hours. I would be down off the coke by then.

A commuter train was blocking the intersection, so I turned down the frontage road next to the train track. Just as I made the turn, I noticed a car following me. I saw the passengers arm reach out the window and put a red flashing light on the top of the undercover car. They got out and approached my car cautiously.

The big undercover cops badge was on his belt. He stood next to my car and asked, "Can I see your license and registration?"

I slowly reached into the glove department for my paper work, while the other cop watched from the passenger side.

"Would you please get out of the vehicle sir?"

I stepped out of the car and stood there with the big cop, as the other officer went to run my license through the system in the patrol car. I noticed the passengers in the stopped train all staring at me. I was getting nervous, as I was starting to get high from the line of coke I had snorted five minutes ago.

The big cop asked me if I had ever been arrested before. I told him of the two joints I had been arrested for in the sixties. He asked me if I was ever convicted of a felony. I told him that back then it was a felony. He was surprised. He said he was just a kid back then.

His partner returned and reported the findings to him. He looked at me while holding my license and said, "Your license is expired due to a failure to appear for a fixit ticket in San Francisco last year."

"Oh, that ticket. I just got the tail light fixed so I could go take care of that tomorrow."

They looked at each other, stepped back and talked to each other secretly.

"My partner seems to think that you appear to be nervous and sweaty. Are you on meth?"

I thought to myself, 'why did I do that line of coke?'

I answered them. "No, I'm not on speed. In fact, I'm on my way to an AA meeting right now."

They had another secret talk. I couldn't believe that I might get arrested for being under the influence. The big cop looked at me and said, "My partner and I think you're high on meth."

I truthfully assured them I was definitely not on meth.

"You mean to tell me if we take you down to the station and drug test you, there will be no meth in your system?"

"I definitely am not on meth. It will just be a waste of your time… and I will miss my AA meeting."

"Well, we believe you are on meth, so we are going to take you downtown to get tested."

I couldn't believe they were going to arrest me. Here I am trying to get sober, and I snort that stupid line of coke. The train left the station. I was glad that the train full of people was not going to watch me get arrested. Who knows who was on that train?

Suddenly, as they were getting the handcuffs out, they got a call for and armed robbery at the liquor store down the street. The big cop yelled to me as they sped off, "This is your lucky day!"

I couldn't believe it. I drove home, and nervously paced back and forth in my kitchen… like a caged lion. When it was time for AA, I was such a mess I couldn't go. I couldn't wait for the coke to wear off. I started worrying about losing my day job delivering auto parts if didn't get my license soon. I smoked a joint to calm myself down. I was a worried mess.

The next morning, I awoke to my sister calling. I rolled out of bed and answered the phone.

"Hi sista'. What's up?"

"Did you go to a meeting and find a sponsor last night?"

'No, I couldn't go."

"Why not?"

"I snorted a line of coke and got pulled over by some under-cover cops. I almost got arrested. They ran a check on me and my license is suspended. I think I will lose my delivery job if they find out. I'm afraid to drive anywhere. I have a failure to appear warrant out of San Francisco."

"OK Mark, here's what you need to do. Are you working today?"

"No, it's my day off."

"Get one of your friends to give you a ride down to the court, and take care of that warrant. You need to get it straightened out so you can get your license reinstated. Pay the fine, get an abstract, and go down to the DMV and get your license back."

"I don't know if I can do all of that today."

"Just do it. Do the footwork. Call one of your friends to give you a ride, and get it done. You need to keep your day job. OK?"

"Alright, I'll get started."

"Oh, and then go to a meeting and find a sponsor. You need to work those 12-steps to get your life back together. I'll call you tomorrow."

After talking to my sister, I felt like just giving up. But I knew she would call again, and again, and again; until I was working the program. The program had already saved her and my brother. I made the coffee and started doing what I needed to do. I couldn't just give up. It took me all day in the court house and the DMV, but I got my license reinstated. That night I went to a meeting.

There was a man at AA who was talking about getting five DUI's. He went to prison for a felony DUI because someone was seriously injured. I thought about how that could have happened to me. I told the group I felt lucky because of the thousands of times I drove under the influence, and I never got a DUI.

After the meeting, someone came up to me. He said he heard me say, I was lucky I didn't get a DUI. He thought that if I would have gotten a DUI a long time ago, I probably would have stopped drinking sooner.

My way of thinking was definitely being challenged the more I went to AA. I kept going because they said if you keep coming back, you will eventually hear someone share a story that you can really relate to.

I was going to meetings every night, looking for a sponsor so I could tell my sister I had one. I kept asking women, but they told me they don't sponsor men.

It was the 22nd of January and I had about 25 days without a drink, and two weeks since I stopped doing coke. I was getting ready to go to an AA meeting that night. I smoked a couple of joints with my friends, still partying in my kitchen. I asked them if they wanted to go with me. They just looked at me like I was crazy.

When I got to the meeting, the speaker was a long haired, old hippy type a guy. He talked about selling acid and mushrooms back in the Haight Ashbury days of the sixties. He had been clean and sober for 5 years and just comes back to share at meetings about his journey. When he mentioned drugs, a few of the 'old timers' in the room got up grumbling about these people talking about drugs at AA meetings. He also said he was a recovered alcoholic, which was unacceptable. You were supposed to say 'recovering alcoholic.'

None of this bothered me because I could totally relate to his story. After the meeting, I stayed around talk to him about being my sponsor. He seemed cool enough to understand me. When he was through talking to quite a few people, he noticed me just standing there against the wall. He looked over my way and said, "Are you looking for a sponsor."

I looked around to see if he was talking to someone else. I was the only one there.

He walked toward me and replied, "I'm looking for a sponsee to work with so I can remain sober; do you have a sponsor?"

I couldn't believe he was asking me. I hesitatingly answered him. "No I don't have one. I'm looking for one."

He put his hand on my shoulder and said, "Let's get some coffee and go talk about it."

We sat down at a table and he started out by saying, "I noticed that you smell like pot, and you look stoned. Do you know what clean and sober means?"

I told him, "I haven't had a drink or snorted coke for a couple of weeks, but I smoke pot every day."

He kind of chuckled a little, and then seriously stated; "If I'm going to be your sponsor, you have to quit smoking pot too. You need to be clean and sober."

I couldn't believe it. My brother had told me the same thing. I really wanted this guy to be my sponsor, but I didn't think he would mind if I still smoked pot. I didn't really want to quit, but I said I would stop. I asked him when he wanted to start working with me and he said, "Right now!"

"Right now? I left my Big Book at home."

"That's OK, we will just do the first three steps tonight; then you can bring your book tomorrow night and we will continue. Do you know what the first step says?"

There happened to be the twelve steps hanging on the wall behind him. I didn't have the steps memorized, so I read the first step.

"Step one is: We admitted we were powerless over alcohol and that our lives had become unmanageable."

He gave me a look like he knew I was reading it off the wall.

"So, are you ready to take that first step?"

"To tell you the truth, this is my 3rd or 4th time coming to AA, and I never really thought my life was unmanageable. I considered myself to be a 'functional alcoholic,' but now I am sure it has become unmanageable. I can no longer deny it"

"Yes, our denial keeps us from admitting that first step. Alcohol is a drug, and some of the 'old timers' don't like it when I talk about drugs here. You can replace the word alcohol with any addiction to use the 12-steps. Just remember that being 'clean and sober' means, not being under the influence of any mind-altering drugs. That is why you need to stop smoking the marijuana too. Now what is the second step?"

"Step two is: Came to believe that a Power greater than ourselves could restore us to sanity."

"Do you believe that?"

"Definitely"

"What is your Higher Power?"

"Last month, over Christmas, I prayed to God to help me quit drinking. I finally realized I needed a Power greater than myself. I had lost all of my sanity, and I felt totally helpless."

He took a sip of his coffee. I had never told anyone before about how I felt. He didn't seem to be surprised. He put his coffee cup down and looked me straight in the eyes and said: "That is why most people are in these rooms. You are not alone. There is hope in these rooms for us alcoholics and addicts. Now what is the third step?"

"The third step is: Made a decision to turn our will and our lives over to the care of God as we understood Him."

He looked at me and smiled. "Are you ready to do that?"

"I have heard in these rooms that God could and would if He were sought. I have asked him on my knees to help me."

"Excellent. We must surrender our self-will to win with the care of God. They are going to close this place so I will meet you tomorrow night, and we will start step four. Thank you for doing this step work with me."

I went home, happy that I could finally tell my sister that I had found a sponsor, and, had worked the first three steps. My fear of getting a sponsor was over. Now I had to tell my friends I am quitting pot too.

I walked up the back stairs to my apartment. I could smell the marijuana smoke floating out the kitchen window. I opened the door where the party was on.

"Well, I found a sponsor, and he said I need to quit smoking pot too."

They all looked at me with a shocked, surprised look. My roommate exhaled the big hit of marijuana he had just taken.

"What, are you kidding me? Alcohol is your problem, not pot!"

"I've tried the program stoned before. It doesn't work that way. I need to do the program the way it is suggested."

My friend Big Mikey reached into his shoebox full of marijuana buds and pulled out the best one. He rolled it into one big joint with six cigarette papers. He looked at me and said, "Well if your serious good buddy, I saved the best for last."

I felt like I was at a farewell party. I had been partying with these guys for many years. This was the final party. Eventually they all stopped coming over to my kitchen to party all night long.

I still see the blind drummer occasionally, and Big Mikey got in the program after he got busted big time and faced prison. He was too unhealthy to go to prison, so the judge released him to an inpatient program. He remained clean and sober, and became a minister until he died of a heart attack. He had a big heart; but not big enough to make it to fifty years old. Most of my other friends that partied like I did died before they reached recovery.

When I got into recovery, I always heard that if we went back out there, the only things awaiting us were jails, institutions and death. It proved to be true for my generation of friends and acquaintances.

That was twenty years ago. When I finally got a couple of years of sobriety and got my sanity back, I heard a man share at a meeting. He really knew what he was talking about. After the meeting, I asked him how he knew so much about addiction. He told me he went to a community college and studied for a couple of years to become a certified drug and alcohol counselor. I decided that night that I wanted to be a counselor like him.

I became a drug counselor, anger management counselor, domestic violence counselor, dual diagnosis counselor and finally... a DUI counselor. When I ended my 17-year career as a counselor, I was working with prisoners in the California Department of Corrections, doing therapy groups with felons.

When I was in college, the director of the Substance Abuse Counselor program told us, "You all will be the example of hope that your clients and patients need to see. When they see how you were able to change your lives, it will give them the hope to change theirs."

The main lesson I tried to teach in my DUI classes and groups was, that whether you are an alcoholic or addict, or just a social user, you are all at risk for going to jails, prisons and institutions. I lived my life 'at risk' for many years, and drove as a dangerous drunk and under the influence. As long as we continue to choose this risky behavior of driving under the influence, we risk losing everything, and we endanger innocent victims by our bad behaviors. We all need to be aware of the consequences of our bad behaviors, and change them through knowledge of how to change. If we need help to change, the help is out there waiting for us to ask for help. Just remember that the decision is yours to make. These can truly be life and death decisions! You can improve the quality of your life.

A Time to Heal.
Turn! Turn! Turn!

ABOUT THE AUTHOR

Retired substance abuse counselor Mark Lashley has taught thousands of people in California DUI programs. In addition to being a substance abuse counselor, he has been in recovery for over twenty years. Lashley writes from a deep place of understanding, having lost his son to a fatal DUI accident. *DUI & You & Me: Save Lives* is his first book.

Made in the USA
San Bernardino, CA
08 September 2017